Make the Grade in GCSE

German

TEACH YOURSELF BOOKS

An audio-cassette has been produced to accompany this course and is available separately via all good bookshops or, in case of difficulty, direct from the publishers.

For further details please write to the publishers at the address given on page iv, enclosing an SAE and quoting Teach Yourself Books (Dept. MtG/F/Cass.).

Make the Grade in GCSE

German

Rod Hares

TEACH YOURSELF BOOKS
Hodder and Stoughton

For Pauline, Antonia, Gareth, Jackie, Julia and Kate.
With special thanks to my friends Rita Clarke, Konrad and
Thea Böse and family, the good people of Büdingen,
Werner and Anne-Marie Schneider, who gave so freely of
their time and kindness.

First published 1989

Copyright © 1989
Rod Hares

No part of this publication may be reproduced or transmitted in
any form or by any means, electronically or mechanically,
including photocopying, recording or any information storage
or retrieval system, without either the prior permission in
writing from the publisher or a licence, permitting restricted
copying, issued by the Copyright Licensing Agency,
33–34 Alfred Place, London WC1E 7DP

British Library Cataloguing in Publication Data
Hares, R. J. (Rod J.)
　Make the grade in GCSE German.—(Teach Yourself books)
　1. German language—For schools
　I. Title
　438
ISBN 0 340 42873 2

Printed in Great Britain for
Hodder and Stoughton Educational,
a division of Hodder and Stoughton Ltd.,
Mill Road, Dunton Green, Sevenoaks, Kent,
by Richard Clay Ltd, Bungay, Suffolk

Photoset by Cotswold Typesetting Ltd., Gloucester

CONTENTS

Introduction vii

Listening 1
1 Eating out
2 Food and drink
3 Finding your way
4 Public transport
5 Shopping
6 Accommodation
7 The railway
8 On the telephone
9 Minor illness
10 Weather and numbers
11 Conversations
12 Radio commercials
13 TV reports
14 People talking I
15 People talking II

Reading 33
1 Cafés and similar places
2 Looking at print
3 Onion sauce
4 More snacks
5 Shop signs
6 Places to stay
7 Emergencies
8 Warning notices
9 Small ads
10 Following directions
11 Two letters
12 Television programmes
13 Steffi and Boris
14 Agony Uncle

Speaking 61
Role-play 1: Saying goodbye
Role-play 2: At the customs
Role-play 3: At a camp-site
Role-play 4: At a garage
Role-play 5: Asking your way
Role-play 6: Shopping
Role-play 7: At the post office
Role-play 8: Public transport—the railway station
Role-play 9: Public transport—the underground
Role-play 10: At a restaurant
Role-play 11: Reporting lost property
Role-play 12: Arranging to meet someone
Role-play 13: At the doctor's
Role-play 14: At the cinema
Role-play 15: Ordering a snack
Role-play 16: At the service station

General conversation 78
1 Ihr Informationen zu Ihrer Person und Ihrer Familie
2 Ihr Alltag
3 Zu Hause
4 Ihre Interessen und Hobbys
5 Ihre Bildung
6 Das Wetter
7 Die Ferien
8 Im Ausland
9 Eine Zeitfrage
Situation narrative 1
Situation narrative 2

Writing 97

1 Postcards 1
2 Diary
3 Postcards 2
4 Postcards 3
5 A holiday invitation
6 Postcards 4
7 Postcards 5
8 Booking accommodation
9 Postcards 6
10 Writing to an information office
11 Telling a story 1
12 Tellng a story 2
13 Telling a story 3

Language points 120

German–English Vocabulary 143

INTRODUCTION

The GCSE German course tests you in the four separate skills of Listening, Reading, Speaking and Writing.

How to use this book

The book is divided into four main sections, following the way the GCSE examines separately the four skills of Listening, Reading, Speaking and Writing. There is also a section of grammar notes, for reference, and a comprehensive vocabulary.

Do not work all the way through one skill, then proceed to another: work on all four skills, a little at a time.

First, work out with your teacher whether you are likely to be entered for the basic or for both levels in a particular skill. Then follow these guide-lines:

Basic Level: Work through each skill section to the double line (e.g. to the end of p. 26 in the Listening Comprehension Section).
Higher Level: Work right through each skill section to the end.

All the texts for the Listening Comprehension work (pp. 1–32) will be found in the book. However, these extracts and much of the Speaking work have also been recorded on a supplementary cassette.

Listening (pages 1–32) Do not work through too much material at a time. Look at the extract twice, or better still, find someone to read it out to you—perhaps a friend or a parent. If you have the supplementary cassette, listen to a taped exercise twice (more often in the early stages) and perform the tasks required, then look through the printed version of what you have heard, listening to the tape version at the same time. Check the things you found difficult, writing down the points if necessary. Look at or listen to the material again the next day. This time, you should aim to understand and remember the meaning of at least three quarters of it.

If you have access to the cassette, listen to it while ironing, washing up, putting on your make-up, gardening, doing the housework, etc., until you are completely familiar with it.

Reading (pages 33–59) Once you have decided the level towards which you are working, tackle the exercises in small but regular doses. If you have a cassette-recorder, it may help you a great deal to speak many of them onto tape and then to play them through.

Once you have been through all the exercises, go back through them again. This second time, aim for eighty to ninety per cent correct understanding.

The Listening Comprehension extracts can also be used as reading exercises. Since the GCSE syllabus is based on the idea of survival in *practical* language situations in German-speaking countries, you will find that much of the material for Listening and Reading Comprehension is very similar.

Speaking (pages 61–95) Follow the same pattern as with your Listening work. Find someone—a friend, parent or better still someone who speaks good German—to practise with you. Repeat the material in the exercises sentence by sentence and get used to speaking out loud.

If you have the cassette, play through the material section by section until you know it backwards. Try to find alternative ways of giving many of the answers. Find a voice on the tape which you like. Try to imitate it. Become familiar enough with this voice for it to keep coming back to you at odd times during the day. When you begin to feel you know the material, stop the tape after each sentence or long phrase and repeat what has just been said.

Writing (pages 97–119) Work through the exercises appropriate to your chosen level. Come back to each exercise after an interval and practise it again. Note how much improvement there has been since the first time.

For those exercises where a key is inappropriate, ask your German teacher or someone else with competent written German if he or she would be prepared to check what you have written.

Before the exam

1 Advance preparation
In the last weeks before the exam, revise the material you have practised during the year. Pay particular attention to the corrections, additions and improvements marked on your work by your teacher. Try to find the time to do again some of the year's less successful exercises.

2 Pair work
It will often help to get a friend of similar ability to your own to work through class material and parts of this book with you. This is particularly true of your oral work.

3 Over- and under-working
It is impossible to lay down the exact amount of time an individual should spend on revision, but there is a general rule of thumb concerning Modern Language learning which we will do well to remember: material learnt gradually is remembered more effectively than material learnt in lengthy periods of cramming very close to the exam date.

In the month before the exam, most students will get restless and will feel worried to a greater or lesser degree. You cannot tell people not to worry, and when you have an important hurdle in front of you a little adrenalin is no bad thing. However, there are things you can do to channel your nervous energy productively. Try to meet a target of 2–3 hours' revision a night, averaging 18–20 hours over a week and dividing your time fairly amongst your various subjects.

If you are doing less than 18–20 hours a week studying for a full range of subjects during that last month, then you know you have to increase your work-rate. However, it is often just as unwise to overwork. For most people, more than a regular 3 hours a night is too much. Try to have a break in the middle of the evening and avoid going to bed immediately you finish your evening's work.

If you normally like to go out two or three evenings a week, then you may well be able to do more than 3 hours on the remaining evenings. If you are working very hard, you should set aside some time for leisure. You learn better if you can come back to your work fresh from a short absence.

4 Realistic self-assessment and targets
Most of the time, we have a fairly accurate idea of our abilities, but with exam subjects, we may sometimes think we are very much better at our work than we actually are. Here, your teacher can be of great help. He or she will tell you how you are likely to do in German. Armed with this knowledge, set yourself a target of one grade above this (unless, of course, you are predicted to get a Grade A). Work to that level, one grade above expectations (see the section *How to use this book*), and be determined to achieve it. This should allow you a safety net, i.e. with a little good fortune, if you fall short of your target, it will only be by one grade.

5 Self-organisation
There are other ways you can organise yourself, besides keeping to your schedules.

(*a*) *Classify!* Keep a file for your revision notes. Divide it into the four skills: 1 Listening, 2 Reading, 3 Speaking and 4 Writing. Additionally, file all corrected work and hand-outs which you have received from your teacher(s) under the four sections. This will help you see very clearly your relative strengths and weaknesses, simply by looking at your marks and corrections, section by section.

(*b*) *Materials* If you are not too short of money, it is worth investing in good standard notebooks, files, document wallets, pens, pencils, etc. Try to have your more necessary materials always to hand, so that you can work neatly, check references and save time by not having to hunt for materials before you start an evening's work.

6 Eye- and ear-memory
The memory relies on a mixture of both the eye and the ear, but for most of us, one will be more important than the other when it comes to remembering. Ask yourself whether you learn better by seeing things written down or by hearing them spoken.

If you learn more effectively from what you have heard, and you have access to a cassette, try to tape as much as you can of the more difficult reading material with which you have to deal.

If you find the printed word easier, ask your teacher if you can see a copy of a listening text after you have worked through it.

In this book, you will find a printed version of all spoken material. If you learn better by ear, don't be afraid to speak the reading material onto tape and to play it back.

The day of the exam

1 *The night before* You yourself know how you sleep best. Perhaps you need to be physically tired from sport, or you fall asleep after a few pages of an enjoyable novel, or after eating a lot! Try to get as good a sleep as you can, but don't fall into the trap of going to bed hours before your normal time; it seldom works!

2 *The morning itself* Try to follow your normal routine, i.e. no heavy breakfast if you normally just have a cup of tea. Make sure you arrive at the exam hall in good time.

3 *The exam room* Take a watch or small clock with you, so you can divide your time sensibly. Make sure your materials are in good order—no blunt pencils or leaking pens—and set them out neatly on your table or desk.

4 *The exam paper* The pace of the Listening Comprehension and the Oral Exam is determined by the tape and the examiner respectively. However, you have control over the pace of your Reading Comprehension and Writing Paper. Read through each paper briefly and calmly before you start writing, so that you will have some idea of what lies ahead and can make a reasoned choice from any options. After you have completed the paper, give yourself time at the end to check through for errors and omissions.

Individual papers

The listening comprehension The teacher/supervisor should ensure that:

1 All windows are closed.
2 The tape-recorder is placed so that all candidates can hear it properly.
3 Necessary proper names are written on a board.
4 The beginning of the tape is played to make sure that 2 is complied with.

If any of these is accidentally forgotten by your supervisor, ask politely for it to be done (omitting any one of these four points can affect your performance significantly).

Before the test begins, try to be as calm as you can. Listening comprehension is traditionally a test in which a significant proportion of candidates let their nerves get the better of them, and for understandable reasons. None of us likes being dependent on a mechanical device. Breathe deeply and remember that all questions carry the same weight, so that if you have missed or not understood a question, all is not lost. Try to put the offending question out of your mind and listen for the next one.

Introduction xi

You can prepare effectively for the listening test by:

(*a*) obtaining the recommended tape which supplements this book and playing it as frequently as possible, so that you begin to know it backwards;
(*b*) aiming to be able to answer most questions after the first hearing, so that you can use the second hearing for filling the gaps;
(*c*) following the hints given on p. 1, and the tips given with individual exercises;
(*d*) learning the vocabularies;
(*e*) listening for voice cues (see p. 1).

The reading comprehension The set time for this test will usually be between 25 and 40 minutes. Most candidates find they are given enough or even ample time. Try to adopt the following pattern when completing a reading comprehension exercise:

1 Except with the individual short questions, read through the whole of the material in an exercise before attempting to answer it.
2 Answer those questions you find easy or you can reasonably cope with first, and come back to the more difficult ones afterwards.
3 Don't be too put off if you can't answer a question. One or two extremely difficult questions are often inserted in both the Listening and the Reading Comprehension, so that anyone obtaining full marks will have earned them! The question you find bewildering may well be that almost impossible one.
4 With multiple-choice questions, look for the most *reasonable* answer. Don't be temped to choose something that might be right only from a sarcastic point of view.
5 In the year preceding the exam, learn the vocabularies in this book.

The oral exam Most of the exam skills needed are discussed on pp 61 and 78–9. Try to bear in mind the following:

1 Be polite and pleasant.
2 Try to keep the conversation flowing by giving answers which are not just a short phrase or sentence. Don't be afraid to put two or three sentences together.
3 In general conversation, have the courage to ask the odd question of the interviewer.
4 If you are at a loss for a word and are stuck,
    (*a*) try to change the direction of the conversation, or
    (*b*) ask for the word in German.

To prepare yourself for the oral exam, practise the questions and answers or play through the oral tape frequently until you begin to know the relevant material backwards. Get someone who speaks good German to practise it with you.

The written paper(s) For most people, this is the biggest hurdle. It will often determine whether the most able candidates will get a Grade A, B or C. As with the other papers, study and exam skills for this test can be acquired long before you actually sit it.

To make the most of your potential, remember the following pointers:

1 Stick closely to what is asked of you (e.g. if you are asked to write something 100 words long, *don't* make it 70 or 150 words).
2 In particular, do not write too much. The number of words demanded of you in a set time is usually as much as can be reasonably expected of a candidate. So if you write in excess of the required word total, you will be reducing your chances of doing well, since more errors will automatically creep in and . . .
3 Silly errors do not help you. Train yourself to look for these unforced errors and to eliminate the majority of them.
4 Make sure that where more than one piece of information is required, you have included the correct number of items.
5 Set aside the last ten minutes of your time for checking through your work for errors.
6 Write your German on alternate lines, so that there is more space in which (*a*) to spot your errors and (*b*) to put in neat corrections.
7 When you receive a corrected piece of work from your teacher, write out the correct version of those sentences or long phrases in which you had errors.

Targets

Each of the four skills of Listening, Speaking, Reading and Writing counts for twenty-five per cent of the total marks for the level. You will need to score around eighty per cent of the marks available in the work in a particular skill (sometimes called a *domain*) to get the complete points allocation for that section.

Please ask your teacher to explain this, as it can be rather complicated.

Because the purpose of this book is to help you *make the grade*, some of the work you do will be a little harder than the work you will actually come across in the exam. This is deliberate, to try and give you something of a safety net.

Viel Glück!

Rod Hares

LISTENING

No matter how strong a candidate you may be, you are unlikely to perform well if you do not listen carefully to what you hear. There are many key words and phrases for which you need to listen, since they form patterns, and these will often help you decipher bits of speech which might otherwise escape you.

Here is a short list of some of the more common key material. Make your own list of further common patterns of speech as you work through the book.

If you see . . .	*it tells you:*
-geschäft	*some sort of shop/place where things are made*
offen/geschlossen	*open/closed*
verboten	*something is not allowed*
örtlich	*local/belonging to the town*
Hilfe	*emergency or help*
im Notfall	*in an emergency*
außer Betrieb	*out of order/broken down*
zu mieten	*for hire*
zu verkaufen	*for sale*
kostenlos	*something is free of charge*
gebührenpflichtig	*a charge will be made*
eingeschlossen	*something is included in the price*
Nachname . . . Vorname	*surname . . . Christian name (=family name . . . given name)*
bei . . . melden	*you need to sign in, report somewhere*
Fußgänger-	*something about pedestrians*
ausgenommen	*except for*
bzw (= beziehungsweise)	*and/or*
möglichst . . .	*as . . . as possible*
falls	*in case*

Voice cues

You can learn a lot from the sound of the voices. When listening to extracts in German, try to work out whether the people sound angry, cheerful, miserable, bored, enthusiastic, frightened, excited, etc. If you can work out the mood of the speakers, it may sometimes be enough for you to answer the question correctly!

LISTENING
1 Eating out

Aufgabe 1 Match each statement with the correct short conversation:

(a) The young man chooses a very popular prawn dish.
(b) The waiter asks if they would like anything else to drink.
(c) They all order tomato soup as a starter.
(d) The service charge is included.
(e) The diner asks for hotpot.
(f) It's up to the customer whether or not to tip.
(g) This person chooses fruit salad.
(h) It's difficult to choose if you haven't been given a menu!

Answers: (a) 5, (b) 8, (c) 1, (d) 6, (e) 3, (f) 7, (g) 4, (h) 2.

Aufgabe 2 √ oder × ?

Each English statement refers to the German conversation of the same number. Place a √ or a × by the statement, according to whether you think it is right or wrong.

 9 They are discussing the desert.
10 They wonder whether they should leave a tip.
11 The waitress is asking for the meal ticket.
12 Hopefully, the waiter is about to bring the cheeseboard.
13 The man has had enough to eat, without actually enjoying it.
14 The meal was first-class.
15 Apple strudel is off the menu.

Answers: 9 ×, 10 ×, 11 √, 12 √, 13 ×, 14 √, 15 ×.

Eating out 3

1   M: Schönen guten Abend, die Herrschaften! Was darf es sein?
    F: Dreimal Tomatensuppe als Vorspeise, bitte.

2   F: Haben Sie schon gewählt?
    M: Noch nicht, wir haben keine Speisekarte!

3   M: Ich hätte gerne einen Eintopf, bitte.

4   F: Für mich wäre ein Obstsalat eine gute Idee!

5   M1:   Was dürfen wir für den jungen Herrn tun?
    M2:   Einen Krabbencocktail, bitte.

6   F1:   Ist die Bedienung eingeschlossen?
    F2:   Ja, die Bedienung ist inbegriffen.

7   F: Ist das mit oder ohne Bedienung?
    M: Das liegt bei den lieben Gästen.

8   F: Darf ich den Herrschaften noch etwas zu trinken bringen?

9   F: Was möchten Sie als Vorspeise?

10   M: Und als Nachtisch?

11   F1:   Ich habe mein Essen bestellt!
    F2:   Dann geben Sie mir bitte Ihren Speisebon.

12   M1:   Herr Ober, ich habe das Käsebrett bestellt!
    M2:   Kommt gleich!

13   F: Sind Sie satt geworden?
    M: Ja, ja, es hat auch geschmeckt!

14   M: Hat alles denn den Herrschaften gut geschmeckt?
    F: Ja, prima!

15   F: Dazu haben wir schöne Nachtische zu empfehlen. Heute haben wir einen außergewöhnlichen Apfelstrudel!

LISTENING
2 Food and drink

Aufgabe 1 Listen to the conversations and work out for yourself which are more likely to take place at the counter, and which at a table in a café or snack-bar.

1 ...
2 ...
3 ...
4 ...
5 ...
6 ...
7 ...

Answers: 1 table, 2 counter, 3 table, 4 table, 5 counter, 6 table, 7 counter.

Aufgabe 2 Complete the sentences from the fillers in the box below. Be careful – there are more fillers than you need!

The person is being asked ...

8 for 200 grammes of the other ...
9 for ... butter.
10 for a piece of the ... tart.
11 for the ... of the table.
12 for ...
13 what kind of ... they sell.
14 how much ... they charge.

| knives | larger | liver sausage | each/a piece | cheeseburgers |
| hamburgers | salt | salt-free | spoons | number | letter | forks |

Answers: 8 liver sausage, 9 salt-free, 10 larger, 11 number, 12 spoons, 13 hamburgers, 14 each/a piece.

Food and drink 5

1 F: Ein großes Bier mit Schuß, bitte.

2 F1: Ich hätte gern ein Stück Bienenstich!
   F2: Für achtzig Pfennig ist recht, ja?

3 M: Bitte schön?
   F: Ich möchte einen Kaffee bitte.
   M: Tasse oder Kännchen?
   F: Tasse, bitte.

4 M1: Und für den Herrn?
   M2: Für mich bitte ein Kännchen Schokolade mit Schlagsahne.

5 F: So ein Glas Wein?
   M: Nein größer, bitte.

6 F: Was kann ich Ihnen bringen?
   M: Ich nehme eine Tasse Kaffee.
   F: Und welche Kaffeesorte darf es sein?
   M: Mokka, bitte.

7 F: Zwei Coca Colas, bitte.
   M: Dosen oder Flaschen?
   F: Sie sind zum Mitnehmen. Besser Dosen.

8 F1: Was soll es denn sein?
   F2: 200 Gramm Leberwurst.
   F1: Von dieser?
   F2: Nein, von jener, bitte.

9 M1: Was kann ich für Sie tun?
   M2: Ich hätte gern ein Pfund Butter – salzfrei.

10 F1: Wie kann ich Ihnen helfen?
    F2: Ich hätte Lust auf ein Stück Torte.
    F1: Von dieser?
    F2: Nein, von der großen.
    F1: Setzen Sie sich bitte in dem Saal. Ich bringe es Ihnen sofort.

11 F1: Möchten Sie Sahne dazu?
    F2: Ohne weiteres.
    F1: Wird schnell gemacht. Welche Tischnummer sind Sie?
    F2: Ich habe keine Ahnung. Er ist der in der Ecke.

12 M1: Kommt noch etwas dazu?
    M2: Ich glaube, das wäre alles ... Doch, wir haben keine Löffel!

13 M1: Ja, bitte?
    M2: Wir möchten schnell essen. Was für Hamburger haben Sie?

14 F: Wieviel das Stück, bitte?
    M: Eine Mark vierzig das Stück, liebe Dame!

LISTENING
3 Finding your way

Aufgabe 1 For each of the following pieces of information, find the matching conversation:

(a) There's a multi-storey carpark opposite.
(b) It's second on the right for the Tourist Office.
(c) The place you're looking for is a couple of minutes or so along the street on the left.
(d) It's a short distance on foot.
(e) The savings bank is down the street.
(f) They're round to the left.
(g) It's straight ahead and getting on for a kilometre.
(h) It's right on the corner.
(i) The chemist's is about 5 minutes away.
(j) There's a laundry on the corner of two streets.

Answers: (a) 5, (b) 3, (c) 10, (d) 2, (e) 8, (f) 1, (g) 9, (h) 7, (i) 4, (j) 6.

Aufgabe 2 Fill in the missing places:

11 It's easy to get to the . . . on foot.
12 Don't go up the . . .
13 The . . . is next door!
14 Go right on to the end of the . . .
15 The . . . is on the right immediately after the . . .
16 The . . . is just near by.
17 The . . . is on the left after the . . .
18 The . . . is near (next to) the restaurant.
19 It's opposite the . . .
20 To get to the . . . it's right, then third left.
21 Take this . . .

Answers: 11 sports-centre, 12 cul-de-sac, 13 clinic, 14 one-way street, 15 drug-store (non-dispensing chemist's), bridge 16 underground, 17 open-air pool, traffic island, 18 disco, 19 department store, 20 pedestrian precinct, 21 street.

1   M1: Entschuldigen Sie, wo sind die Toiletten?
    M2: Hier gleich links rum.

2   F1: Ist das Krankenhaus sehr weit?
    F2: Nur fünf Minuten zu Fuß.

Finding your way 7

3 M: Entschuldigung, wo ist hier ein Informationsamt?
   F: Zweite Straße rechts.

4 F: Wo gibt es hier eine Apotheke, bitte?
   M: Am Rathausplatz, ungefähr fünf Minuten von hier.

5 F1: Wo kann man hier gut parken?
   F2: Hier im Parkhaus gegenüber!

6 M1: Verzeihen Sie, bitte, gibt es hier in der Nähe eine Wäscherei?
   M2: An der Ecke Drosselgasse – Hauptstraße befindet sich eine.

7 F1: Wo kann ich hier eine Bank finden?
   F2: Direkt an der Ecke.

8 F: Wie komme ich zur Sparkasse, bitte?
   M: Fahren Sie die Straße runter.

9 M: Verzeihung. Wie komme ich am besten zum Revier?
   F: Zur Polizei? Ach so, Sie gehen immer geradeaus, so ungefähr sieben, achthundert Meter.

10 F: Kennen Sie den Wienerplatz?
   M: Sie gehen diese Straße entlang, 2 oder 3 Minuten, dann finden Sie ihn auf der linken Seite.

11 M1: Wo finde ich die Fußgängerzone?
   M2: Hier rechts, dann die dritte Straße links.

12 F1: Wo gibt es hier in der Nähe eine Drogerie, bitte?
   F2: Sie gehen über die Brücke, dann gleich rechts.

13 F: Wie komme ich am schnellsten zum Sportzentrum?
   M: Möchten Sie zu Fuß gehen oder mit dem Auto fahren?
   F: Zu Fuß.
   M: Dann ist es sehr leicht . . . Gleich um die Ecke, dann bis zur dritten Ampel. Das Sportzentrum befindet sich da rechts.

14 M: Verzeihen Sie. Ich habe mich verfahren. Ich suche das Freibad.
   F: Ist doch leicht. Fahren Sie noch geradeaus bis zur Verkehrsinsel. Dann sehen Sie das Freibad auf der linken Seite . . . in der Mitte.

15 M: Nehmen Sie diese Straße.

16 F: Fahren Sie weiter bis zum Ende der Einbahnstraße.

17 F: Es ist ja gegenüber dem Warenhaus.

18 M: Die Klinik ist nebenan!

19 M: Die Disko ist neben dem Restaurant.

20 F: Die U-bahn ist ja ganz in der Nähe!

21 F: Nehmen Sie nicht die Sackgasse!

LISTENING
4 Public transport

Aufgabe 1 Match each short conversation on page 11 with the right ticket:

(a) 10-er KARTE KÖLN

(b) KÖLN — BONN Einzel–reise 2.K.1. ‖ KÖLN — BONN Einzel–reise 2.K.2.

(c) KOBLENZ Rückfahrkarte 2.Klasse

(d) *DRESDEN Rückfahrkarte*   *DRESDEN Rückfahrkarte*   *DRESDEN Rückfahrkarte*

Public transport 9

BREMEN

Hin und

zurück

2.Klasse

(e)

MÜNCHEN | **MÜNCHEN**

Rück-   Rück-

reise   reise

2. Klasse   2. Klasse

(f)

TEE

KÖLN

—

MÜNCHEN

HIN

(g)

Answers: (a) 7, (b) 2, (c) 5, (d) 3, (e) 1, (f) 4, (g) 6.

10 Public transport

Aufgabe 2 Match each symbol or sign with the right conversation:

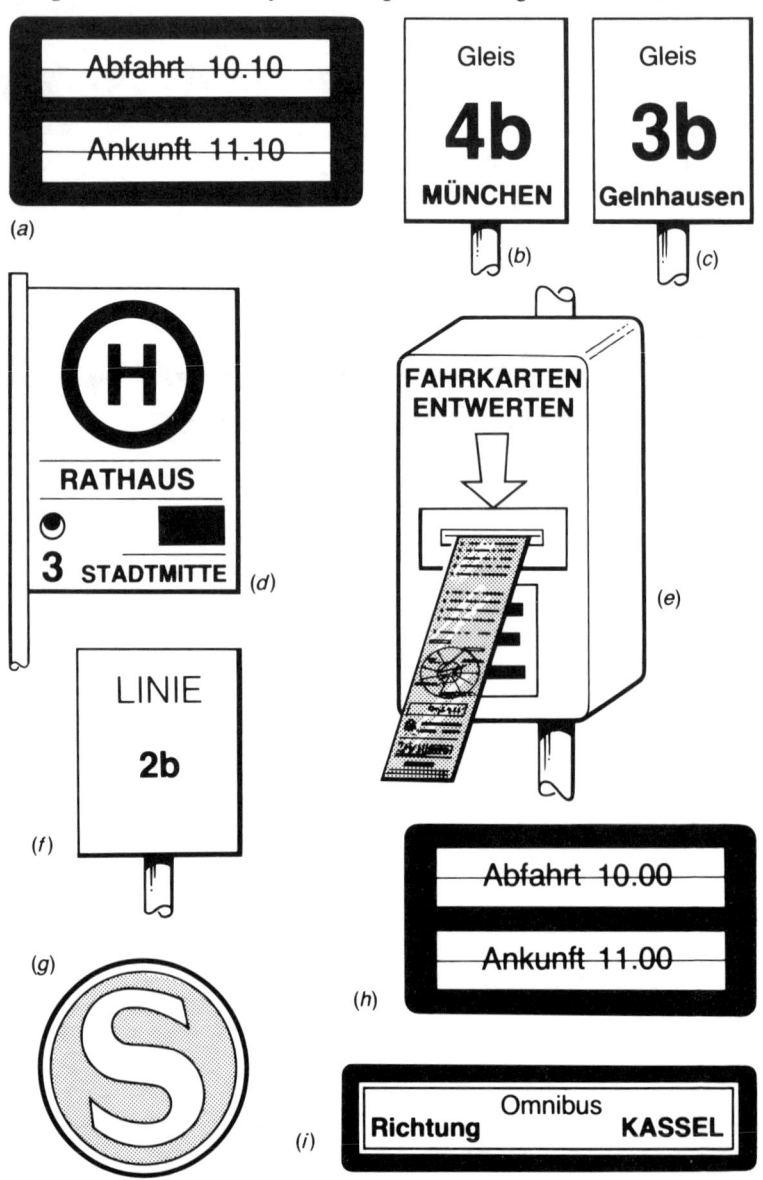

(a) Abfahrt 10.10 / Ankunft 11.10

(b) Gleis 4b MÜNCHEN

(c) Gleis 3b Gelnhausen

(d) H RATHAUS 3 STADTMITTE

(e) FAHRKARTEN ENTWERTEN

(f) LINIE 2b

(g) S

(h) Abfahrt 10.00 / Ankunft 11.00

(i) Omnibus Richtung KASSEL

Answers: (a) 14, (b) 12, (c) 13, (d) 9, (e) 16, (f) 10, (g) 8, (h) 15, (i) 11.

Public transport 11

1 F: Einmal zweite(r) Klasse nach Bremen, bitte, hin und zurück.
2 F: Sie wünschen?
  M: Zweimal nach Bonn, zweite Klasse, nur hin.
3 M: Dreieinhalbmal Dresden, bitte, hin und zurück.
4 F: Zweimal München, Rückfahrkarten.
5 M: Einmal nach Koblenz, hin und zurück, mit Studentenermäßigung.
6 F: Eine Einzelreise nach München, TEE, bitte. Muß ich einen Zuschlag zahlen?
7 M: Eine Mehrfahrtenkarte, bitte, nach Köln-Deutz.
8 M: Wie komme ich am besten zum Stadtzentrum?
  F: Nehmen Sie die S-bahn. Die Haltestelle ist da drüben.
9 F1: Zum Bahnhofhotel, bitte?
  F2: Nehmen Sie die Linie 3 in Richtung Stadtmitte.
10 M: Wann fährt der nächste Bus nach Fulda?
   F: Um 10 Uhr 15, Linie zwo-B.
11 F: Wann fährt der Omnibus nach Kassel ab?
   M: Machen Sie schnell! Er fährt gleich ab!
12 M: Bitte, von welchem Gleis fährt der Schnellzug nach München?
   F: Von Gleis 4B.
13 F: Fährt dieser Zug direkt nach Frankfurt oder muß man umsteigen?
   M: Leider ist dieser Schnellzug nicht direkt. Sie müsen in Gelnhausen umsteigen.
14 M1: Wie lange dauert die Fahrt nach Düsseldorf?
   M2: Knapp eine Stunde.
15 F1: Wann kommen wir in Stuttgart an?
   F2: Um Schlag elf.
16 M: Eine Mehrfahrtenkarte, bitte, und wie gebrauche ich sie?
   F: Sie stempeln die Karte im Entwerter. Ist ja leicht!

LISTENING
5 Shopping

Aufgabe 1 Match each statement with the right conversation:

(a) Opening-time in the morning can vary a little.
(b) The customer gets less than 2 Marks change from a 20 Mark note.
(c) This customer is buying eight stamps.
(d) This customer has a change of mind.
(e) The shop closes at 12 on Saturday.
(f) This gentleman is thinking it over.
(g) This lady will get no change from a 20 Mark note.
(h) This customer doesn't want anything else.

Answers: (a) 8, (b) 6, (c) 2, (d) 1, (e) 7, (f) 4, (g) 5, (h) 3.

Aufgabe 2 Answer in English the questions on the conversations:

9 What affects the time this particular shop closes?
10 For which three things does the customer ask? (3)
11 Explain the problem.
12 What does the cashier say about the change?
13 How much does the time-table cost?
14 How many carnations does the customer buy? What colour are they? (2)
15 Why should the young lady try the other tart? (3)

Answers: 9 How much tourist trade there is. 10 (a) fill-up, (b) check oil, (c) check water. 11 The bill is wrong. 12 It comes out (of the machine) at the bottom right. 13 Nothing – it's free! 14 10, white. 15 (a) the first is rather sour, (b) the other is sweeter, (c) and fantastically tasty.

1 F: Was darf es sein?
   M: 20 Liter ... nein ... für 50 Mark Normal, bitte.

2 M1: Wie kann ich Ihnen helfen?
   M2: Geben Sie mir bitte 5 zu 20 und 3 zu 90.

3 F1: So, bitte. Sonst noch was?
   F2: Ich danke, nein. Das ist alles.

4 M1: Gern geschehen. Haben Sie noch einen Wunsch?
   M2: Ich überlege mal.

5 F: Was macht das wohl?
   M: Genau 20 Mark.

Shopping 13

6 F: Was macht das alles zusammen?
   M: Alles zusammen, sagen wir, DM 18,50.
   F: Da sind 20 Mark.
   M: Und eine Mark fünfzig zurück.

7 M: Wann öffnen Sie am Wochenende?
   F: Nur von neun Uhr bis Mittag.

8 F1: Wann machen Sie an Wochentagen auf, bitte?
   F2: Normalerweise, morgens um halb neun, aber von Zeit zu Zeit ein bißchen später.

9 M1: Und wann schließen Sie?
   M2: Meistens um neunzehn Uhr. Dann und wann etwas früher. Es hängt von den Touristen ab!

10 F1: Kann ich Ihnen helfen?
   F2: Ja, bitte volltanken. Super.
   F1: Gerne .... Sonst noch einen Wunsch?
   F2: Ja, würden Sie bitte das Öl und Wasser prüfen?
   F1: Freilich.

11 M1: 2.60 zurück, danke.
   M2: Tut mir leid, aber das stimmt nicht. Sie haben falsch gerechnet.

12 M: Wieviel schulde ich Ihnen?
   F: 22.80.
   M: Ja, bitte sehr.
   B: Das Kleingeld unten rechts.

13 M: Hier ist ein Fahrplan.
   F: Wieviel, bitte?
   M: Kostet gar nichts. Ist umsonst.

14 F: Ja, bitte?
   M: Ich suche Nelken ....
   F: Welche Sorte, bitte?
   M: Ich hätte gern die weißen Nelken da. 10 Stück, bitte.

15 F1: Eine Obsttorte, bitte.
   F2: Jene ist etwas sauer. Diese ist mehr süßlich und schmeckt unheimlich lecker.

LISTENING
6 Accommodation

Aufgabe 1 Here are some accommodation signs. Listen to the conversations (pages 16–17) and write down the letters of all the signs that fit. Be careful, for there may be as many as four signs matching one or two of the conversations!

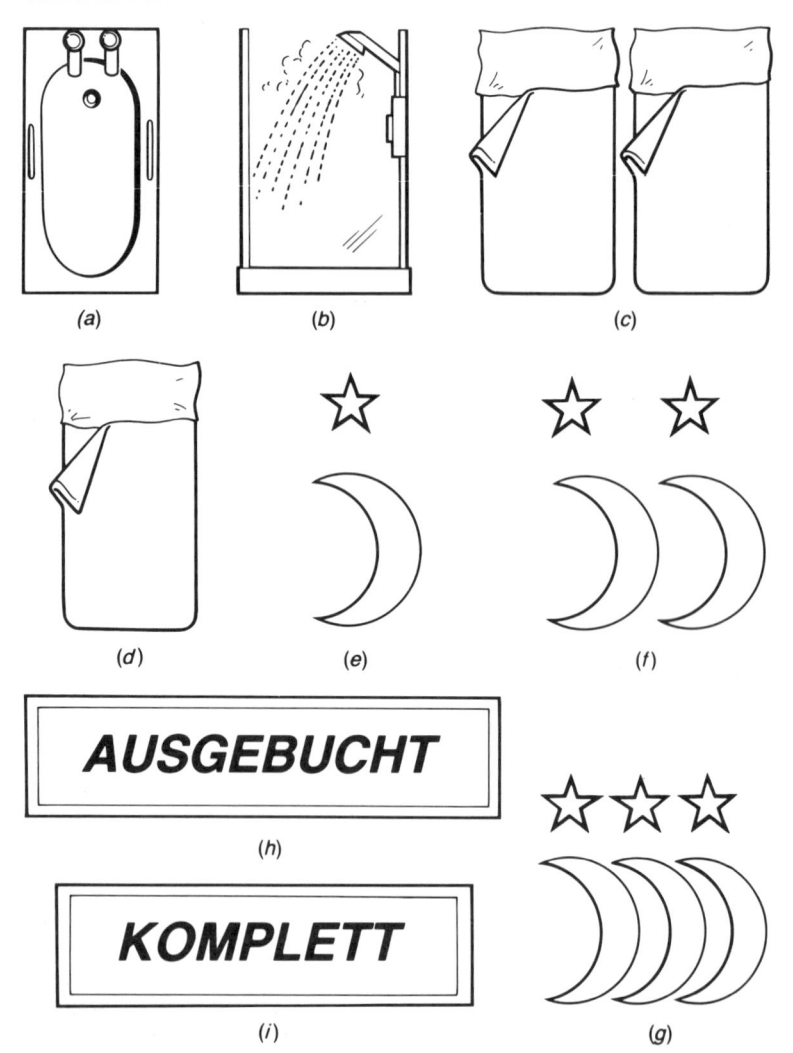

Accommodation 15

Answers: 1 (k), (h) 2 (o), (n), (i), 3 (o), (d), (b), 4 (d), (a), (b), (g), 5 (d), (a), (b), (j), 6 (h), (i), (k), 7 (o), (a), (l), 8 (o), (f), (p), (m), 9 (d), (a), (p).

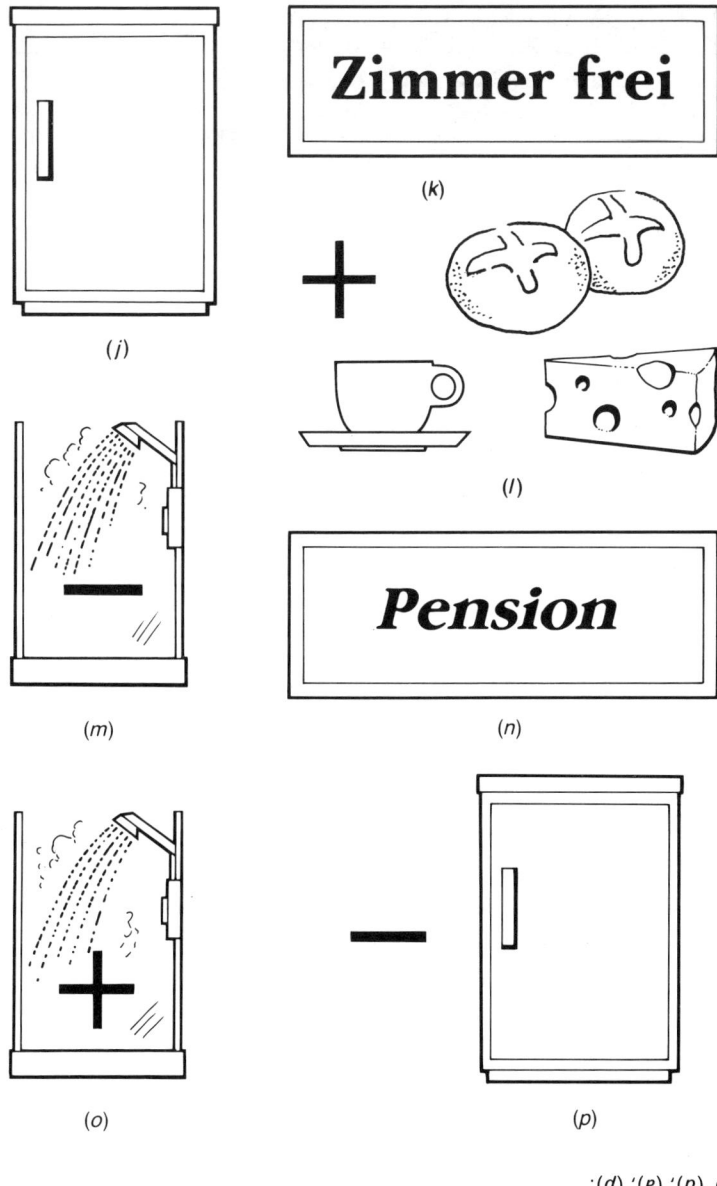

16   *Accommodation*

Aufgabe 2   Richtig oder falsch?
Listen to the conversations and give the statements a √ or a ×:

10   The person is being asked to carry luggage downstairs.
11   The man needs a ball-point to fill in the form.
12   The person has already been given the key for Room 336.
13   Herr Thomas had forgotten he was in Room 281.
14   The lift is outside the main hall.
15   There is a reasonably priced restaurant nearby.
16   There is no room at the camp-site 2 km away.
17   The youth-hostellers are foreigners. They need to show their student cards.
18   There is only one caravan berth left and it's next to the shower-block.

Answers: 10×, 11√, 12×, 13√, 14×, 15√, 16×, 17√, 18√.

1   F: Haben Sie bitte ein Zimmer frei?
    M: Tut mir leid, wir sind ausgebucht.

2   M: Ich suche ein Doppelzimmer.
    F: Wie schade, Sie kommen zehn Minuten zu spät! Die Pension ist jetzt ausgebucht.

3   F: Wir möchten bitte hier übernachten.
    M: Was hätten Sie denn gerne, ein Doppelzimmer oder zwei Einzelzimmer?
    F: Ein Zweibettzimmer mit Dusche, bitte.

4   M1: Können Sie uns bitte hier unterbringen?
    M2: Ich kann Ihnen ein Einbettzimmer mit Bad oder Dusche anbieten.
    M1: Toll! Mit Bad, bitte.
    M2: Und für wie lange wäre das?
    M1: Kommt darauf an . . . sagen wir für mindestens drei Tage.

5   F: Und was für ein Zimmer möchten Sie?
    M: Zwei Einzelzimmer – eins mit Bad, eins mit Dusche und beide mit Kühlschrank, wenn möglich.

6   M: Ich habe leider keine Zimmer mehr. Das Hotel da vorne hat noch Zimmer.

7   M: Möchten Sie das Doppelzimmer mit Bad haben?
    F: Was kostet dieses Zimmer?
    M: 70 Mark inklusive Frühstück.

8   M1: Ich brauche ein Doppelzimmer für zwei Nächte.
    M2: Einen Moment. Kann ich nicht machen. Wir haben nur zwei Einzelzimmer übrig. Das eine ohne Dusche.
    M1: Die nehmen wir.

Accommodation 17

9 F: Ein Einzelzimmer mit Bad, das ginge. Aber leider ohne Kühlschrank.
   M: Macht nichts. Das Zimmer nehme ich, bitte.

10 F1: Würden Sie sich bitte eintragen?
    F2: Ja, gerne, aber wo?
    F1: Hier unten.

11 F: Ihren Paß, bitte, und könnten Sie mir dieses Formular ausfüllen?
   M: Ohne weiteres, aber darf ich Ihren Kugelschreiber borgen?

12 F: Und welche Nummer hat das Zimmer?
   M: Sie haben Nummer 326 in der dritten Etage. Ich gebe Ihnen den Schlüssel. Angenehmen Aufenthalt!

13 M: Ich habe meine Zimmernummer vergessen. Ich bin im zweiten Stock. Ich bin Herr Thomas.
   F: Herr Thomas . . . ach, ja . . . Hier ist Ihr Schlüssel, Nummer 218.

14 F1: Und gibt es auch einen Aufzug?
    F2: Hmm. Es gibt ja einen Fahrstuhl . . . der ist aber außer Betrieb!

15 M1: Können wir auch hier essen?
    M2: Hier nicht, aber es gibt ja ein preiswertes Restaurant nebenan.

16 F: Haben Sie noch Platz?
   M: Leider nicht. Es gibt aber einen anderen Campingplatz nur zwei Kilometer von hier.

17 M1: Ein Bett und einen Schlafsack, bitte. Ich möchte drei Nächte bleiben.
    M2: Wird gemacht. Ich brauche aber Ihre DJH-Karte oder Ihren Studentenausweis, wenn Sie Ausländer sind.

18 F1: Ich suche einen Platz, bitte.
    F2: Für Zelt oder Wohnwagen?
    F1: Für unseren Wohnwagen.
    F2: Für Wohnwagen ist nur ein Platz übrig und der ist neben dem Waschraum.

LISTENING
7 The railway

Aufgabe 1 You are listening to the intercom announcements at a German railway-station. Answer the questions below, as if you were helping other English-speakers who know no German:

1 What is the announcer asking passengers in the arriving train to do?
2 Give three pieces of information about the Kiel train. (3)
3 (a) Which kind of train is referred to?
  (b) Has it come from, or is it going to Cologne?
  (c) Which platform is mentioned?
4 Find out three details about the train at Platform 1A. (3)
5 (a) Why does the announcer's voice sound slightly urgent?
  (b) What are passengers requested to do?
6 (a) Why does the announcer sound apologetic? (2)
  (b) Explain the announcer's suggestion. (2)
  (c) How does the announcer finish what he has to say?
7 (a) Give details of the reason for this announcer's urgent tone. (4)
  (b) What are the passengers requested to do?

Answers: 1 To leave the train. 2 Fast train, leaves Platform 3B, in 5 mins (at 13.37). 3 (a) Inter-City express; (b) come from; (c) Platform 12. 4 Trans-Europe Express, to Bonn, via Aachen and Cologne. 5 (a) Ludwigshafen express from Platform 9; (b) close all doors. 6 (a) Kassel train has been cancelled, because of mechanical difficulties; (b) Take fast train at 19.25, from Platform 4B; (c) by apologising. 7 (a) the fast train to Stuttgart, from Platform 3, at 14.19 is no longer straight through; (b) Change trains at Frankfurt.

Aufgabe 2 Now listen to three short conversations and decide whether the following statements are *richtig oder falsch*. Give each statement a √ or a ×.

8 (a) There is no room in the dining-car.
  (b) The person asks if there are any couchettes available.
  (c) There are none.
9 The person is enquiring about connections to Göttingen.
10 (a) The inspector is checking sleeping-car tickets.
  (b) These passengers only have one between them.
  (c) They should be careful not to fall out of their bunks.

Answers: 8 (a) ×, (b) √, (c) ×. 9 √. 10 (a) √, (b) ×, (c) ×.

The railway 19

1 F: Hauptbahnhof Aachen, Hauptbahnhof Aachen. Bitte aussteigen.

2 M: Der Schnellzug nach Kiel fährt in fünf Minuten um 13 Uhr 37 von Gleis 3B ab.

3 F: Der Inter-City-Schnellzug aus Köln kommt auf Gleis 12 an.

4 M: Der TEE nach Bonn auf Gleis 1A fährt über Aachen und Köln.

4 F: Achtung! Achtung! Der Express nach Ludwigshafen auf Gleis 9 fährt gleich ab. Bitte die Türen schließen.

6 M: Wegen mechanischen Schwierigkeiten fährt der Zug um 19 Uhr nach Kassel nicht ab. Passagiere werden gebeten den Eilzug um 19 Uhr 25 auf Gleis 4B zu nehmen. Diese Veränderung tut der Deutschen Bundesbahn sehr leid.

7 F: Achtung! Achtung! Der Schnellzug nach Stuttgart um 14 Uhr 19 Gleis 3 ist nicht mehr direkt. Reisende nach Stuttgart werden gebeten, in Frankfurt umzusteigen.

8 F1: Der Schlafwagen ist belegt.
   F2: Dann haben Sie keine Liegeplätze frei?
   F1: Doch.

9 M: Habe ich dann Anschluß nach Göttingen?

10 M1: Darf ich Ihre Schlafwagenkarten sehen?
    M2: Wir haben gar keine!
    M3: In diesem Fall können Sie nicht hier schlafen.

LISTENING
8 On the telephone

Aufgabe 1 You are staying with a German-speaking family and have to take a phone message for them, since there is no one else in. Listen carefully to the person on the other end of the phone and work out the following details in English:

1 Who is the caller?..
2 Their reasons for phoning?...(2)
3 Their suggestion?...(2)
4 Why don't your hosts need to worry?..
5 Note the last, very important part of the message ....(2)

tips!
1 There are *two* ways of identifying the caller. You only need *one*.
2 Look for both the reason and what has caused it.
3 The two parts of the suggestion come very closely together.
4 *Worry* links with the key-word *Angst*.
5 This question shows how you need to know your times of the day, week etc.

Answers: 1 Frau Schneider *or* Erika's mother. 2 Have visitors, can't go out with Mr and Mrs Hartmann the day after tomorrow. 3 They go to the theatre next Wednesday. 4 The Schneiders have already seen to the tickets. 5 If the Hartmanns can't come, Frau Schneider must know by tomorrow morning at the latest.

Ach, ja . . . Sie sind auf Urlaub hier bei Hartmann. Würden Sie bitte Frau Hartmann diese Botschaft geben?

Ich bin Frau Schneider, die Mutter von Erika. Übermorgen können wir nicht mit Herrn und Frau Hartmann ausgehen, da wir Besuch haben. Ich schlage vor, wir gehen nächsten Mittwoch zusammen aus, und zwar zum Stadttheater.

Sagen Sie ihr auch bitte, sie sollten sich keine sorgen machen. Ich habe die Eintrittskarten besorgt[1]! Wenn sie nicht kommen können, muß ich spätestens morgen früh Bescheid wissen[2]. Vielen Dank!

[1] *besorgen* to deal with, see to. [2] *Bescheid wissen* to know what's going on.

Aufgabe 2 Your German hosts, short of time, have left a message for you on cassette. Note as much of the following information as you can in English:

1 Why your host is not there..(2)
2 Host's reason for leaving you a message...(3)
3 List the items needed...(4)
4 Where is the money?..(2)
5 How much should be taken and why?..(2)

tip!

In Q3, the speaker continues talking for a while in between mentioning items 3 and 4.

Answers: 1 Tina has called. Host must collect her from train. 2 Shops may be closed before her return; needs a few things urgently from the supermarket. 3½ lb of butter, 6 eggs, cheese, parsley. 4 Up in the little box in the kitchen. 5 30 Marks, that will be enough.

Hallo, Pat! Es tut mir leid, hoffentlich kommst du rechtzeitig zurück. Tina hat angerufen ... aus Gelnhausen ... ich muß sie vom Zug abholen. Ich fürchte, bevor ich zurückkomme sind die Geschäfte geschlossen. Könntest du mir einen Gefallen[1] tun? Ich brauche dringend[2] noch ein paar Sachen aus dem Supermarkt ... Nimm dir einen Bleistift ... Danke ... Jetzt geht's los ... Achtung ...
... Ein halbes Pfund Butter
    sechs Eier
    etwas Käse (such' dir welchen aus, den du gern ißt)
... da war noch etwas ... ich hab's vergessen ... ach, ja ... Petersilie[3].
Bitte, nimm Geld von uns, du weißt ja wo es liegt, oben im kleinen Kästchen[4] in der Küche. Nimm etwa dreißig Mark mit. Das wird reichen ... Danke.

[1]*der Gefallen* favour. [2]*dringend* urgently. [3]*die Petersilie* parsley. [4]*das Kästchen* small box.

Aufgabe 3 You are round at a friend's in Germany. Your own host phones to let you know that there has been an important phone-call for you. Listen to what he says and make a list of all the main points.

tips!

(a) Do you really need to write out Ann's address?
(b) Notice how the speaker's voice tails off at the end. In that case, do you think his last comment is an important part of the message?

Answers: Ann Jones has called. Pat is to phone back to Bridgend 0656 56814. The code for Great Britain is 0044. She has won a big prize in the lottery (5 points).

Hallo, Pat! Stell'dir vor[1], Ann hat angerufen ... Ann Jones, 15, Main Street, Bridgend, 0656 56814. Übrigens[2] ist die Vorwahl[3] für Großbritannien 0044 ... Und was so wichtig ist, sie will dir etwas sagen ... Sie hat in der Lotterie gewonnen und es ist ein größerer Gewinn ... du sollst zurückrufen ... äh ... freu' dich mit ihr.

[1] *sich vorstellen* to imagine. [2] *übrigens* incidentally, by the way. [3] *die Vorwahl* STD code.

LISTENING
9 Minor illness

Aufgabe 1 In conversations 1–5, a patient is talking with a receptionist about a possible medical or dental appointment. Find out in which conversation the patient . . .

(a) says (s)he has an appointment.
(b) has never had an appointment at the surgery before.
(c) can see the doctor up to 6.30 pm.
(d) can be fitted-in for the day after tomorrow.
(e) is expected, and asked to take a seat.

Answers: (a) 3, (b) 5, (c) 2, (d) 1, (e) 4.

Aufgabe 2 Listen to conversations 6–12 between patients and their doctor/dentist/chemist, and fill in the appropriate information on the grid in English:

Conversation No.	Symptoms	Diagnosis	Treatment
6			
7			
8			
9			
10			
11			
12			

Minor illness 23

No. Conversation	Symptoms	Diagnosis	Treatment
6	headache, sweating, sore throat, cough	a cold	—
7	toothache	bad tooth	must come out
8	pain everywhere, high temp., shivers	'flu	prescription, go to bed
9	painful skin	sunburn	prescribes cream, no sun tomorrow, stay indoors
10	unable to sleep	—	tablets
11	pain	wasp sting	antiseptic cream
12	headaches	heat	tablets 3 times a day, with water, before meals

Answers:

1 F1: Ich möchte bitte einen Termin für übermorgen ausmachen.
  F2: Ja, ja, das ginge.
  F1: Wann soll ich dann da sein?

2 M: Ich möchte bitte einen Termin mit der Frau Doktor für Freitag aus machen.
  F: Ihre Sprechstunden sind von 3 Uhr 30 bis 6 Uhr 30.

3 F1: Ich möchte den Doktor sehen.
  F2: Bitte, haben Sie einen Termin?
  F1: Ja, um halb fünf.

4 F: Das ist in wessen Namen?
  M: Im Namen Robert.
  F: Ach, ja, Herr Claus Robert. Bitte, setzen Sie sich da drüben.

5 M: Ich brauche dringend einen Termin mit Herrn Doktor Brandt.
  F: Waren Sie schon einmal bei uns?
  M: Noch nicht. Ich bin Feriengast hier.

6 F: Wie kann ich Ihnen helfen?
  M: Mir geht es nicht gut.
  F: Können Sie mir Ihre Symptome beschreiben?
  M; Ich habe Kopfschmerzen, ich schwitze, der Hals tut mir weh und ich huste.
  F: Lassen Sie mich bitte Ihren Hals sehen . . . Klar . . . Sie haben eine Erkältung. Es ist doch nicht so schlimm.

7 M1: Was ist denn los, junger Mann?
  M2: Ich habe Zahnschmerzen, hier unten.
  M1: Ach, ja . . . Der muß 'raus.

24 *Minor illness*

8 F1: Wo tut's denn weh?
   F2: Ein bißchen überall. Ich habe Fieber und ich zittere.
   F1: Lassen Sie mal sehen ... So, so. Sie haben eine Grippe. Ich verschreibe Ihnen ein Rezept und Sie gehen sofort ins Bett!

9 F: Wo tut es Ihnen weh?
   M: Es ist meine Haut, Frau Doktor.
   F: Das kann ich leicht sehen! Sie haben einen Sonnenbrand. Ich verschreibe Ihnen eine Creme. Und Morgen-keine Sonne! Bleiben Sie drinnen!

10 F1: Es fällt mir schwer, einzuschlafen.
   F2: Diese Tabletten kann ich Ihnen empfehlen.

11 M1: Ich habe einen Wespenstich. Haben Sie etwas dagegen?
   M2: Diese Wundcreme ist ein wirksames Heilmittel.

12 F: Bei dieser Hitze habe ich immer Kopfschmerzen!
   M: Ich gebe Ihnen diese Tabletten. Nehmen Sie sie bitte dreimal pro Tag mit Wasser, und zwar vor dem Essen.

LISTENING
10 Weather and numbers

The weather and numbers are two areas of language that you are sure to have to understand and/or be able to use during your GCSE Tests. This exercise gives you listening practice in both of them.

Auftrag Listen to the taped voice of the weather announcer giving the weather and temperature in various major cities round the world. Fill in for each city on the grid, the letter of the matching weather symbol, plus the correct temperature. Helsinki has been done for you.

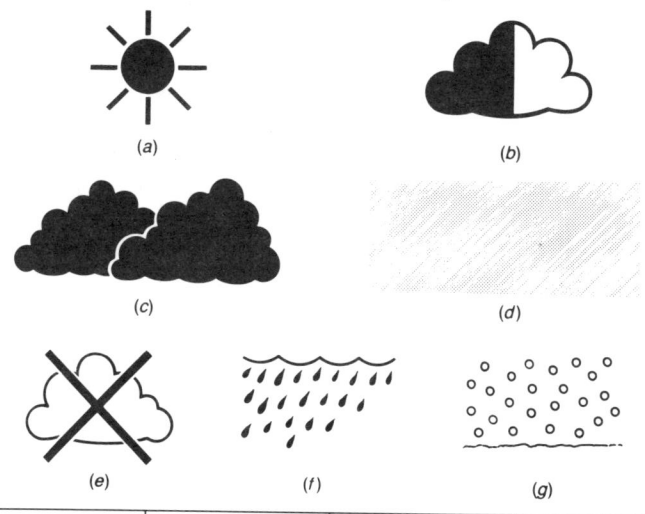

(a)

(b)

(c)

(d)

(e)

(f)

(g)

Helsinki b7	Stockholm	Oslo	Dublin..............
London............	Kopenhagen	Amsterdam	Ostende............
Brüssel	Zürich	Locarno	Paris................
Bordeaux	Nizza................	Barcelona.........	Madrid.............
Mallorca..........	Malaga.............	Lissabon	Wien ....
Innsbruck	Prag	Warschau.........	Budapest..........
Belgrad	Dubrovnik	Bukarest	Konstanza ....
Varna...............	Bozen...............	Venedig............	Rom ....
Neapel.............	Athen	Istanbul............	Leningrad ....
Moskau............	Las Palmas......	Algier	Tel Aviv...........
Kairo	Tokio	Peking...............	New York........

Weather and numbers

Wetter und Temperaturen in Grad Celsius vom Mittwoch, 10 Uhr

Ausland					
Helsinki	wolkig	7	Warschau	bedeckt	1
Stockholm	heiter	7	Budapest	bedeckt	1
Oslo	wolkig	7	Belgrad	bedeckt	6
Dublin	bedeckt	9	Dubrovnik	Regen	6
London	bedeckt	8	Bukarest	wolkenlos	9
Kopenhagen	bedeckt	8	Konstanza	wolkenlos	7
Amsterdam	bedeckt	4	Varna	bedeckt	10
Ostende	Nebel	4	Bozen	wolkig	8
Brüssel	bedeckt	3	Venedig	bedeckt	10
Zürich	bedeckt	2	Rom	bedeckt	16
Locarno	Nebel	9	Neapel	wolkig	18
Paris	heiter	1	Athen	heiter	19
Bordeaux	wolkig	5	Istanbul	wolkig	13
Nizza	bedeckt	16	Leningrad	bedeckt	9
Barcelona	wolkenlos	12	Moskau	Schnee	−3
Madrid	heiter	7	Las Palmas	heiter	21
Mallorca	heiter	16	Algier	heiter	18
Malaga	heiter	17	Tel Aviv	heiter	16
Lissabon	heiter	13	Kairo	heiter	17
Wien	bedeckt	3	Tokio	bedeckt	18
Innsbruck	heiter	1	Peking	bedeckt	11
			New York	heiter	8

END OF BASIC WORK

LISTENING
11 Conversations

Sometimes, a conversation can continue for quite a long time without telling you very much, perhaps because one of the speakers is not very talkative by nature, or a little shy. This is just such a conversation.

Auftrag Your task on this occasion is to listen to the dialogue as often as you need, and to put together the smaller pieces of information so that you build up something of a picture of Christine. For example, it is not enough to find out that Christine is a housewife – she is something else, as well.

tips!
1 *Der Drahtesel* is a disco in Büdingen. It is directly opposite the police-station!
2 *Compound nouns* are those nouns that have (at least) two parts to them like *Deutschlehrer/Fußballspielerin*. If they crop up in your listening work and you've not heard them before, try to separate the two halves. You may recognise one or both of them and that will help you put together the two ideas that give you the new word. In this conversation, listen for the following compound words. We've separated the halves to help you:

   Gymnasium/straße . . . Spazieren/gehen . . . Ein/kaufen . . . Winter/club . . . Industrie/gebiet . . .

   Remember, if a longish word is difficult to understand, try to separate the parts that make it up.

Rita: Also, Christine, stell' dich erstmal vor!
Christine: Ich heiße Christine Borowicz und bin 21 Jahre alt.
Rita: Und wo wohnst du genau?
Christine: In Büdingen in der Gymnasiumstraße 25.
Rita: Was bist du von Beruf?
Christine: Ich bin Hausfrau.
Rita: Du bist schon . . . ?
Christine: Mutter.
Rita: Hausfrau und Mutter. Also . . . wie verbringst du deinen Tag zum Beispiel?
Christine: Mmm . . . mit Spazierengehen, Einkaufen . . .
Rita: Gut. Also, wenn man hier etwas vor hat, geht man in *Den Drahtesel* oder kann mann sonst noch woanders hingehen?
Christine: Oder in den Winterclub.
Rita: Wo ist das?
Christine: Oben im Industriegebiet.
Rita: Gut, also auch nur in Büdingen?
Christine: Ja, in Büdingen.

28 Conversations

Rita: Also, du bleibst praktisch in Büdingen?
Christine: Ja.
Rita: Wo warst du letzten Sonntag?
Christine: Da war ich spazieren im Wald.

(9) *Answers:* Christine Borowicz is 21 years old ... she lives in Büdingen ... she is a housewife and mother ... She spends her days going for walks ... and shopping ... Christine goes to the *Drahtesel* disco ... and to the *Winterclub* for entertainment ... She spends virtually all her time in and around Büdingen ... Last Sunday she went for a walk in the local woods.

LISTENING
12 Radio commercials

Listen to the radio commercials as often as you feel necessary. Then answer the questions below:

1. (*a*) What is on special offer at *Leder-Vater*?
   (*b*) Find both the original and the sale price. (2)
   (*c*) You wish to inspect the bargains at *Leder-Vater*. Which two streets on the Frankfurt map have a branch of the store? (2)
2. (*a*) Find the name of the item being advertised.
   (*b*) What kind of thing is it?
   (*c*) How much does it cost?
   (*d*) Name the two selling points mentioned in the commercial. (2)
3. (*a*) What does the product want to tell you about itself?
   (*b*) How do the sound effect and the music fit in with the last part of the commercial?

1. Bei *Leder-Vater* im Angebot, Herren und Damen – Lammpelze, statt 1500 jetzt 890 Mark.
   Leder-Vater, Frankfurt – Hauptwache und Kaiserplatz.

2. *Bild-Woche* – was braucht man mehr?
   Ja, was braucht man mehr als *Bild-woche*, die Programm-Illustrierte – aktuell und preiswert, nur 90 Pfennig.

3. *Licher-Bier* will Ihnen, ohne viele Worte zu verlieren, etwas über seine Herkunft sagen.
   Licher-Bier – aus dem Herzen der Natur!

Answers: 1 (*a*) Sheepskins, (*b*) Original cost – 1500 marks, now reduced to 890 marks, (*c*) The Hauptwache and Kaiserplatz. 2 (*a*) Bild-Woche, (*b*) Illustrated TV magazine, (*c*) 90 pfennig, (*d*) Up-to-date/good value. 3 (*a*) Where it comes from, (*b*) They give an impression of nature and the countryside. (12)

LISTENING
13 TV reports

Listen to these brief excerpts from German television and use the hints below to help you answer the questions:
1 Find the two main facts in this short newsflash.
2 Find as many details as you can about tomorrow's weather.

Tips!
1 If a longish word is difficult to understand, it may split up into two words you know quite well. There are two examples here: *Staats . . . chef, Oppositions.- . . führerin.*
2 Remember that the word *aber* often suggests a contrast, e.g. *this may be the case, BUT.*
3 You know *nebelig trüb* from the reading material on page 00. If you don't understand *heiter*, remember that *teils . . . teils* (partly . . . partly . . .) is likely to bring together two opposites.

1 Hier ist das *Erste Deutsche Fernsehen* mit der Tagesschau[1]. . .
Guten Abend, meine Damen und Herren! Mehr als 2 Millionen Menschen haben in der philippinischen Hauptstadt Manila gegen Staatschef Marcos demonstriert[2].
Die Oppositionsführerin Aquino rief[3] zum gewaltlosen[4], aktiven Widerstand[5] gegen die Regierung auf.

2 Die Vorhersage für morgen . . .
Im Norden und Osten vielfach[6] stark bewölkt, aber nur vereinzelt[7] etwas Schneefall . . . Sonst, teils heiter teils[8] nebelig trüb und trocken.
Tiefsttemperaturen, minus 4 bis minus 9 Grad.

[1]*die Tagesschau* (lit. "The Daily Show") a news magazine programme. [2]*demonstrieren* to demonstrate. [3]*auf-rufen* to call for. [4]*gewaltlos* peaceful, [5]*der Widerstand* opposition. [6]*vielfach* (in) many different (areas). [7]*vereinzelt* occasional, scattered. [8]*teils . . . teils . . . partly . . . partly.*

Answers: 1 There has been a very large demonstration in Manila against Philippines' President Marcos. Opposition leader Aquino has called for peaceful non-cooperation. (2). 2 A great deal of cloud in the North-East . . . with scattered falls of snow . . . Otherwise, sometimes sunny (cheerful) . . . foggy . . . overcast . . . dry . . . Lowest temperatures will be in the range -4 to $-9°C$. (7)

LISTENING
14 People talking I

Anne-Marie is talking about her sporting interests. Listen for the following precise details. The tips below should help you.

1 Find all four sports in which Anne-Marie takes part. (4)
2 Find two words in the text that go with *langsam* and *schnell*. (2)
3 How many times a week does she play in summer? (2 possibilities)
4 What do you learn about *Völkling* at the end of the conversation? (2)

tips!
1 When you are looking for the sports, listen for action-words following closely on *ich*.
2 *langsam* and *schnell* must refer to music or dances.
3 Here, *in der Woche* means *on week-days*.

Rita: Anne-Marie, kannst du mir sagen, welchen Sport du treibst?
Anne-Marie: Ja, mehrere Sportarten! Ich schwimme gerne ... ich spiele gerne Tennis ... des öfteren fahr' ich rad und ich tanze sehr gern ... wenn man das als Sport bezeichnen[2] will.
Rita: Natürlich kann man das als Sport bezeichnen. Welche Tänze zum Beispiel tanzt du am liebsten?
Anne-Marie: Alle Arten von Tänzen – langsame sowohl wie[3] schnelle ... das kommt darauf an[4] ... auf die Stimmung[5].
Rita: Und welche Musik magst du am liebsten um danach zu tanzen?
Anne-Marie: Das kommt darauf an ... mal schnelle, mal langsame. Das ist wie ich sagte ... Ich liebe den Tango genau so gut wie ein Diskosound.
Rita: Hmmm ... ist interessant ... Können wir noch mal auf Tennis zurückkommen?
Anne-Marie: Ja.
Rita: Wie oft spielst du Tennis?
Anne-Marie: Im Sommer spiele ich mit Sicherheit[6] zweimal in der Woche und am Wochenende ... eigentlich[7] Samstag, Sonntag.
Rita: Und hast du einen besonderen[8] Tennisschläger ... welche Marke ist denn dein Tennisschläger?
Anne-Marie: Ich habe einen *Völkling*.
Rita: Ist es eine deutsche Marke?
Anne-Marie: Er ist in Deutschland sehr bekannt[9], aber ob er deutsch ist, weiß ich gar nicht.

[1]*Sportarten* kinds of sport. [2]*bezeichnen* describe, call. [3]*sowohl wie* as well as. [4]*das kommt darauf an* it all depends. [5]*die Stimmung* mood. [6]*mit Sicherheit* certainly. [7]*eigentlich* actually, really. [8]*besondern* special. [9]*bekannt* well known.

LISTENING
15 People talking II

(Peter Thienel has hypnotised a patient, who is recounting what appears to be her previous life in prehistoric times.)

Listen to the conversation and then answer the questions:

1. How does Barbara describe the picture right at the beginning? (2)
2. Describe the scene as soon as everything becomes clear. (3)
3. What does Barbara say about the opening?
4. What kind of people does she see?
5. Why can't Barbara say how old she is?
6. What does Barbara see once Peter Thienel has snapped his fingers? (3)
7. How does Barbara look in relation to the others?
8. What is Barbara's main daily tasks?
9. Describe what it is like inside the dwelling. (2)
10. How do the men occupy themselves during the day? (2)
11. Describe what they bring back. (3)

Answers: 1 Getting brighter, looks like fog. 2 High cliffs, grass growing, caves in cliffs. 3 You get to the cave through it. 4 Ape-like (Neanderthal) people. 5 She can't see herself. 6 She has big feet, looks funny, hair all over, except her front. 7 Just like them. 8 To fetch grass to keep fire burning. 9 A fire always burning in the middle, otherwise quite cold. 10 They fetch water, and fruit from afar. 11 Fruit like yellow, shiny peaches, taste very sweet with no stones.

Thienel: Was siehst du jetzt?
Barbara: Nichts.

Es vergehen weitere Minuten, in denen sich nichts tut. Barbara schweigt. Doch plötzlich sagt sie: Es wird heller, sieht aus wie Nebel.

Thienel: (*energisch*) Geh da durch!
Barbara: Jetzt wird alles ganz deutlich und klar. Ich sehe hohe Felsen. Es wächst Gras. Man kann überall längslaufen. In den Felsen sind Höhlen. Man gelangt durch eine kleine Öffnung hinein. Ich gehöre hierher.
Thienel: Sind da Menschen?
Barbara: Nein, keine richtigen Menschen, affenartige Gestalten, die liegen in der Höhle. Wir sind Neandertaler.
Thienel: Wer bist du? Wie siehst du aus? Wie alt bist du?
Barbara: Weiß ich nicht. Ich sehe mich gar nicht.
Thienel: Ich schnippe mal mit dem Finger, dann siehst du dich. Schau an dir herunter.
Barbara: Ich sehe meine großen Füße. Komisch. Da sind Haare dran. Aber auch an den Beinen, Armen und ma Rücken. Nur vorne sind keine. Ich bin ein Mädchen, habe nichts an.
Thienel: Bist du hübsch?
Barbara: Ich sehe aus wie alle.
Thienel: Hast du Eltern?
Barbara: Hier sind so viele Alte. Ich weiß nicht, ob ich Eltern hab'.
Thienel: Was machst du denn tagsüber?
Barbara: Gras holen, damit das Feuer nie ausgeht. Es brennt immer, mitten in der höhle. Denn hier drinnen ist es sonst ganz kalt. Draußen aber ganz warm. Wir schlafen am Feuer, auf Gras oder Fellen. Um die rötlich-braunen Felsen herum ist es hart, nur Gras und Gestrüpp.
Thienlel: Wie alt bist du denn?
Barbara: Das weiß ich nicht, bin noch jung.
Thienel: Was gibt es bei euch zu essen? Und was zu trinken?
Barbara: Die Männer besorgen Früchte und Wasser. Das Wasser tragen sie in braunen oder schwarzen Fellen nach Hause. Die Früchte sammeln sie von weither. Sie sehen aus wie gelbe blanke Pfirsiche, schmecken ganz suß, haben aber keine Kerne. Und dann die großen roten Beeren, die schmecken so ähnlich wie Kirschen, haben auch keine Kerne.

READING

Many of the skills you have already developed to help you with your Listening will be of considerable use to you for the Reading test, so look back at the hints on p. 1 before attempting this section.

Just as your ear needs to be trained in Listening Skills, in Reading Skills you need to use your eyes. Work through the exercises one by one, until you have reached your top level.

General hints

The Reading papers test your ability to understand those items in German which it is important that you should be able to read when you are actually in a German-speaking country. You may be questioned on material ranging from the briefest of public signs (sometimes only *one* word) to quite long newspaper or magazine articles and reports.

Except for the very short items you will not be expected to understand *every single word* of what you read, although even in the longest tasks, the great majority of the words you will come across should already be known to you from the general vocabulary lists set by your Exam Board. The all-purpose vocabularies at the back of this book are a rough and ready version of those laid down by the different Boards. If you know these, it will stand you in very good stead for the Reading test(s).

However, if you cannot recognise a word, do not let it throw you. Look, instead, at the sentence in which the word appears and at the surrounding few lines. These will often give you some clues to the approximate meaning of the word, and this may be all you need. On the other hand, much of the quite difficult new vocabulary you may come across in, say, a newspaper report, may have no connection with the questions and the answers you are required to give.

With very *short notices* and *signs*, there is a lot you can do to help yourself by remembering important pointers such as the following:

verboten/nicht erlaubt/kein bitte nicht ... unbefugt	*all tell you that something is* not *allowed or* not *recommended*
bei ... melden	*contact ... (for info.)*
parken Parkscheibe Parkhaus Parkscheine	*all have to do with parking*
Hilfe im Notfall!	*refers to some emergency service*

READING
1 Cafés and similar places

Aufgabe Which of the signs below tell you the place to go to if you want . . . :

(a) to sit and take your pick of the ice-cream?
(b) to take your pick of the cream cakes?
(c) a self-service snack bar?
(d) fried or barbecued meals and snacks?
(e) snacks?
(f) a simple meal with something to drink?
(g) to drink beer?
(h) a fried sausage?

1   EISSALON
2   GRILL
3   **WURSTBUDE**
4   **GASTHAUS**
5   *SCHNELLESSEN*
6   SELBSTBEDIENUNG
7   BIERHALLE
8   **KONDITOREI**
9   *EISDIELE*
10 IMBISSSTUBE

Answers: (a) 1 and 9, (b) 8, (c) 6, (d) 2, (e) 5 and 10, (f) 4, (g) 7, (h) 3.

READING
2 Looking at print

Aufgabe Look at the receipt below, and answer the questions.

```
7184    3  27.03.89              10

SP/RUEHREI          6.90
KELLOGGS            1.50
MILCH 0.25          1.40
        ZWI-SU              9.80

        TOTAL               9.80
        (07.45)
```

1 Find out what three things this customer ordered at the service-station and work out approximately how much each cost in English money. (Assume that 3 DM = £1).
2 How much change (in Marks and Pfennigs) would the customer have recieved from a 20 Mark note?
3 Which meal do you think he or she was eating?

Tips!

Q1: The "/" tells you that this is an either or item, so make sure you answer with "either ... or ...". *UE* on bills = *ü*, so the word is *Rührei*. *SP* stands for *Spiegel = Spiegelei*.

Q2: Remember there are 100 Pfennig to the pound, so you take *9.80* away from *20.00*. You are unlikely to get a straight maths question like this, but you should be able to add up and take away in German money.

Q3: Questions like this test your sense of logic. This one is pretty obvious. *Kelloggs* can only mean one thing!

Answers: 1 Scrambled eggs (£2.30), Cornflakes (50p), Milk (47p). 2 10 Marks 20 Pfennig. 3 Breakfast.

READING
3 Onion sauce

Aufgabe 1 You are at a camp-site in a German-speaking country and are the only one in your family who knows any German. Explain, as accurately as possible, to whoever is doing the cooking (it may be yourself), how to prepare the onion sauce. Try to explain all the steps.

Zwiebel-Soße

Mindestens haltbar bis Ende
MAI 87 5LXN

Fein gehackte und geröstete Zwiebeln, verfeinert mit Paprika, Pfeffer und weiteren pikanten Gewürzen, geben dieser Soße ihren besonderen Geschmack.

Besonders geeignet zu:
★ *Leber*
★ *Rostbraten*
★ *Kotelett*
★ *Schnitzel*
★ *Leberkäse*
★ *Bratwurst*
★ *Frikadellen*

Zubereitung:
Beutelinhalt in reichlich 1/4 Liter (300 ml) kaltes Wasser einrühren, unter Rühren aufkochen und bei schwacher Hitze mit etwas geöffnetem Topfdeckel 10 Minuten kochen. Ab und zu umrühren.
Bei Zubereitung von 2 Beuteln nur 550 ml Wasser verwenden.
Auch bei der Mitverwendung Knorr Zwiebel-Soße stets in kalte Flüssigkeit einrühren.

1/4 Liter (250 ml) enthält durchschnittlich:

	Fett			Kilojoule (Kilokalorien)
3,4g	9,9g	21,6g		800 (190)

Zutaten: Röstzwiebeln, Stärke, Rinderfett, Würze, Maltodextrin, Reismehl, Zucker, Salz, Tomaten, Geschmacksverstärker, Hefeextrakt, Gewürze und Kräuter.

C.H. Knorr GmbH, 7100 Heilbronn

23633-0-153-64

Onion sauce

Aufgabe 2 Explain for which dishes the sauce is specially recommended.

Tips!

1. Soup and similar instant-food packets often have a lot more information printed on them than just the cooking instructions. So, don't feel you have to read through *all* the information on the packet. If you have to explain cooking instructions, look for the key-word *Zubereitung* (Preparation), and start there.
2. *Schlüsselwörter: Beutelinhalt* packet contents, *einrühren* stir in, *unterrühren* while stirring, *schwache Hitze* low heat, *der Topfdeckel* saucepan lid, *ab und zu* now and again, *verwenden* use.
3. For Aufgabe 2, look at what is written under the key-phrase *Besonders geeignet zu* (Especially suitable for . . .). You should have come across all these dishes in your German course.
4. Another key-phrase, which may be of use to you on another occasion occurs towards the top of the packet. *Mindestens haltbar bis Ende . . . = best consumed by the end of . . .*

Answers: 1 Stir contents into 300 ml (=300 cc) of cold water. Heat while stirring. Simmer for 10 minutes on a low heat. . . . with the saucepan lid partly open. Continue to stir occasionally. If you are preparing two packets, you only need 550 ml (cc) of water. (6) 2 Liver . . . roasts . . . chops/cutlets . . . escalope . . . (spiced) meat loaf . . . fried sausage . . . rissoles. (7)

READING
4 More snacks

Aufgabe 1 Match these signs with the German ones on the opposite page:

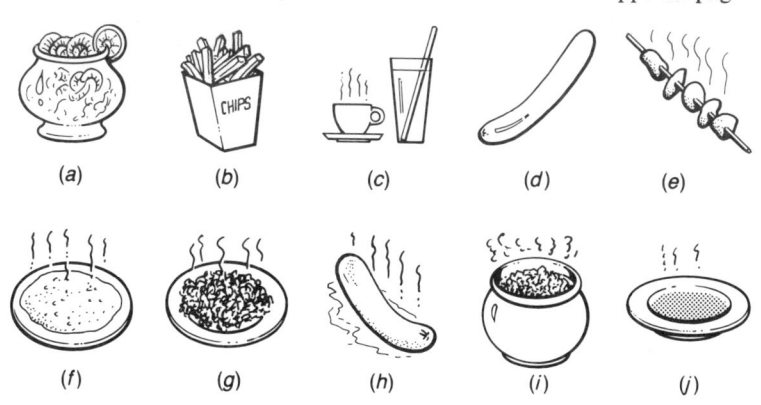

(a) (b) (c) (d) (e)

(f) (g) (h) (i) (j)

Answers: (a) 9, (b) 4, (c) 6, (d) 8, (e) 1, (f) 10, (g) 5, (h) 2, (i) 3, (j) 7.

Aufgabe 2 List the food descriptions in the two boxes opposite under these three headings:

schmeckt   schmeckt nicht   ist unterschiedlich

für Feinschmecker
hausgemachter Art
lieblich
lecker
schmackhaft
wohl riechend
süßlich

zu würzig
zuviel Pfeffer
zu salzig

gepfeffert
sauer schmeckend

Answers:

40 *More snacks*

1. **SCHASCHLIK**
2. *CURRYWURST*
3. EINTOPF
4. POMMES FRITES
5. **HACKSTEAK**
6. *WARME UND KALTE GETRÄNKE*
7. **TAGESSUPPE**
8. BOCKWURST
9. ***KRABBENCOCKTAIL***
10. BAUERNOMELETTE

---

zu würzig
für Feinschmecker
hausgemachter Art
sauer schmeckend
gepfeffert
lieblich

---

lecker
zuviel Pfeffer
schmackhaft
zu salzig
wohl riechend
süßlich

READING
5 Shop signs

Aufgabe   Look at the shop signs below, and answer the questions:

1. Alter signs *b*, *g*, *m*, *q* to fit with the message in Sign *d*.
2. Find all notices which tell you the shop is closed (3). Explain the ways in which they differ.
3. Find all the notices about sales and special offers. Two of these notices have to do with holidays. Find them and explain the difference between them.
4. What is the difference between Signs *l* and *o*?
5. Which three notices have to do with paying and which is the odd-one-out?
6. Which notice could refer to either a trolley or a pen? What is its usual meaning?

Answers: 1 (*b*) 22.00 das Kilo, (*g*) 1.00 die 200 Gramm, (*m*) 3.20 das Stück, (*q*) Statt 12.70 7.92. 2 (*a*), (*h*), (*n*): (*a*) simply says "closed", (*h*) is closed due to illness, (*r*) is closed for the holidays. 3 (*c*), (*d*), (*f*), (*k*): (*c*) advertises holiday prices, (*k*) advertises sale-prices before the management's own Winter holidays. 4 In (*o*) we are told the shop is open all day. 5 (*e*), (*i*), (*j*). (*i*) is odd. The other two tell you where to pay – (*i*) reminds you to keep your receipt. 6 (*n*) Please take a trolley from here.

(*a*) Geschlossen

(*b*) 2.50 das Kilo

(*c*) **Ferienpreise**

(*d*) 20% billiger

(*e*) **Am Ausgang zahlen!**

(*f*) Preis-Zensur

42 *Shop signs*

(g) 1.25 *die* 200 *Gramm*

(h) **Wegen Krankheit geschlossen**

(i) BITTE, IHRE QUITTUNG BEHALTEN!

(j) ***Hier zahlen***

(k) Winterschlußverkauf

(l) **Geöffnet**

(m) **4.00 das Stück**

(n) Bitte Kuli hier nehmen!

(o) *Ganztägig Geöffnet*

(p) **Sonderangebote**

(q) *Statt 9.90!!*

(r) ***Betriebsferien***

READING
6 Places to stay

Aufgabe Match the English signs with the German ones on page 44:

(a) Youth Club

(b) FULLY BOOKED

(c) Hotel/Public House

(d) 3 rooms to let

(e) Youth Hostel

(f) Youth Hostel

(g) Rooms To Let

(h) Tourist Office

(i) Tourist Office

(j) HALF BOARD

(k) YHA

(l) FULL

(m) holiday flat

(n) Green Meadow camp-site

(o) FULL BOARD

(p) GUESTHOUSE

Places to stay

1	Gasthaus	9	*Pension*
2	*Zimmer zu vermieten*	10	**Jugendheim**
3	**Jugendclub**	11	Jugendherberge
4	Informationsamt	12	Ferienwohnung
5	**Verkehrsamt**	13	*Raumangebot: 3 Zimmer frei:*
6	*Camping zur grünen Wiese*	14	**Halbpension**
7	**Ausgebucht**	15	*Voll*
8	Vollpension	16	DJH

Answers: (a) 3, (b) 7, (c) 1, (d) 13, (e) 10/11, (f) 10/11, (g) 2, (h) 4/5, (i) 4/5, (j) 14, (k) 16, (l) 15, (m) 12, (n) 6, (o) 8, (p) 9.

READING
7 Emergencies

Aufgabe Once again, match the English signs with the German ones on page 46:

(a) *Red Cross*

(b) Emergency Telephone

(c) *FIRE-SERVICE*

(d) **Police**

(e) In an emergency contact the police

(f) for emergency use

(g) **Police Station**

(h) *Consultation by appointment*

(i) *Gynaecologist*

(j) ENT Specialist

(k) Emergency Service

(l) *EMERGENCY EXIT*

(m) *Dentist*

(n) Public Health Department

(o) PHYSIOTHERAPIST

(p) *Consultation hours: 2–4.30*

(q) G.P.

(r) HOMOEOPATH

(s) Standby Pipe

(t) *Hospital*

46 Emergencies

1. Frauenarzt
2. Dr H. Hasewinkel, Zahnarzt
3. **Facharzt für Hals-Nasen-Ohren-Krankheiten**
4. Krankengymnastin
5. *Homöopath*
6. **Termine nach Vereinbarung**
7. **Sprechstunden, 14.00–16.30**
8. Praktischer Arzt
9. *Krankenhaus*
10. Gesundheitsamt
11. Polizei
12. *Feuerwehr*
13. *In Not!*
14. Notrohr
15. **Das Rote Kreuz**
16. Polizeiwache
17. *Notausgang*
18. Notrufsäule
19. **Revier**
20. Notdienst
21. **Im Notfall sich bei der Polizei melden**

Answers: (a) 15, (b) 18, (c) 12, (d) 11, (e) 21, (f) 13, (g) 16/19, (h) 6, (i) 1, (j) 3, (k) 20, (l) 17, (m) 2, (n) 10, (o) 4, (p) 7, (q) 8, (r) 5, (s) 14, (t) 9.

READING
8 Warning notices

Like in English, German notices advising, suggesting, or warning you (not) to do something can sound anything between very polite and highly abrupt. Here are a few pointers which will help you find your way through all the warning notices you may come across:

Aufgabe Work out for yourself the meanings of Signs 6–19, using the hints below to help you.

tips!

(a) Signs 1–3 are basic one-word warnings of danger, or of the need for care.
(b) ! If the sign has an exclamation mark, this important piece of punctuation will often tell you that you are being asked (not) to do something.
(c) The use of *bitte* makes a request sound more kindly.
(d) The words *kein, nicht, nur, privat, unbefugt, verboten,* will usually tell you that something is not allowed, or perhaps allowed with strict limitations.
(e) *Falsch, kostenpflichtig* tell you very definitely NOT to do something, because if you do it is going to cost you money!
(f) Signs containing *Hinweise, Anweisung, Gebrauchs-* will normally give you instructions how to do something.

1. Achtung!

2. *Vorsicht!*

3. **Gefahr!**

4. Hinweise

5. **Gebrauchsanweisung**

6. Bitte nicht rauchen!

7. *Bitte Ruhe!*

8. **Besteigen Sie nicht die Brücke!**

48 *Warning notices*

9   MOTORRADFAHREN VERBOTEN!

10 *Parken nur für*
    Fahrzeuge der Firma

11 Privater Parkplatz

12 Parkfläche für Besucher

13 **Kein Eintritt für**
    unbefugte Personen!

14 Gebrauchsinformation-
    sorgfältig lesen!

15 *Falschparker werden*
    kostenpflichtig
    abgeschleppt!

16 Sicherheitzgurt
    bitte anschnallen!

17 **Lebensgefahr!**

18 *Gebrauchsbenutzungen*

19 ZWISCHEN
    2300–700
    NICHT HUPEN!

Answers: 6 No smoking please. 7 Quiet please. 8 Don't go on to the bridge. 9 Riding of motorcycles not allowed. 10 Parking only for company vehicles 11 Private parking-place. 12 Visitors' car park. 14 Instructions for use – to be read carefully. 15 Unauthorised vehicles towed away at owners' cost. 16 Please fasten your safety-belt. 17 Danger! 18 Instructions for use. 19 No horns between 11 pm and 7 am!

READING
9 Small ads

You may be expected to cope with a wide variety of small ads, so look *carefully* at the questions *you* have to ask. They may be just as varied. With longer ads, a careful look at the *English* questions will actually give you quite a lot of information before you start. In Q7, for instance, you know straightaway that the person is looking for a record-player and that it must meet certain conditions.

Aufgabe Study the small ads and answer the questions:

1 For what is this advertiser looking?
2 What is this advertiser prepared to consider, in order to obtain readers' 8 mm films? (3)
3 What is on offer here?
4 For what purpose is a British au-pair required?
5 What is this advertiser keen to exchange for what? (2)
6 (*a*) Does this advertiser wish to *buy* or *sell* a TV set?
   (*b*) What four things do we learn about the set? (4)
7 Which condition does the advertiser lay down about the record-player he is seeking?
8 (*a*) For whom is this advert intended?
   (*b*) Why is Jan–Feb mentioned?
   (*c*) How are the prices described?

1
> Suche:
> Alles über Sting

2
> Möchte 8 mm-Filme kaufen/
> verkaufen/austauschen

3
> Mofa-Ersatzteile 20–30% bil-
> liger!

4

Suche britisches Au-Pair für langfristige Ferienreise nach Indien

5

Tausche Wham-Platten gegen Eintrittskarten fürs Queen-Konzert

6

Tragbarer schwarz/weiß Fernseher, Neuzustand für nur DM 100 – zu verk. Tel. 0641/81484 ab 18 Uhr

7

Suche:
Plattenspieler (Philips) mit Verstärker in gutem Zustand

8

Hallo, Skifreunde! In Bormio/Italien Einzelbett/Doppelbettzimmer frei Jan.–Feb. Günstige Preise.

Answers: 1 Anything to do with *Sting*. 2 Buying, selling, or exchanging. 3 20–30% cheaper moped spare parts. 4 A long holiday trip to India. 5 Wham records for tickets for the *Queen* concert. 6 (*a*) to sell, (*b*) portable, black and white, as new, wants 100 Marks. 7 The amplifier must be in good condition. 8 (*a*) skiers, (*b*) single/double bedroom free, (*c*) favourable.

END OF BASIC WORK

READING
10 Following directions

Aufgabe   You are in Berlin and are stopped by a tourist who does not speak German. She is trying to get to the *Nationalgalerie* at the *Potsdamer Brücke*. Draw for her on the map both of the suggested routes to the gallery, explained below the map.

tips!

When you have to make sense of directions remember that you need to know your place-words. So, it is key-words that are essential to giving and understanding directions. Learn this list of most of the expressions you need to know.

Schlüsselwörter

abbiegen to turn off
die Ampel traffic-lights
der Bahnübergang level crossing
bis until, up to
der Bürgersteig pavement
die Brücke bridge
entlang along
die Fußgängerzone pedestrian zone
der Fußgängerübergang pedestrian crossing
der Fußweg footpath
gegenüber opposite
der Gehweg footpath
der Gehsteig footpath
geradeaus straight on

hinter behind
immer geradeaus keep straight on
die Landstraße road, main highway
links left
neben near, next to
oben up, above
rechts right
die S-bahn tram/metro network
über over
umsteigen to change (buses, etc.)
unten down, below
U-bahn(hof) tube(station)
die Verkehrsinsel roundabout
vor in front of
zum/zur to the.

52 *Following directions*

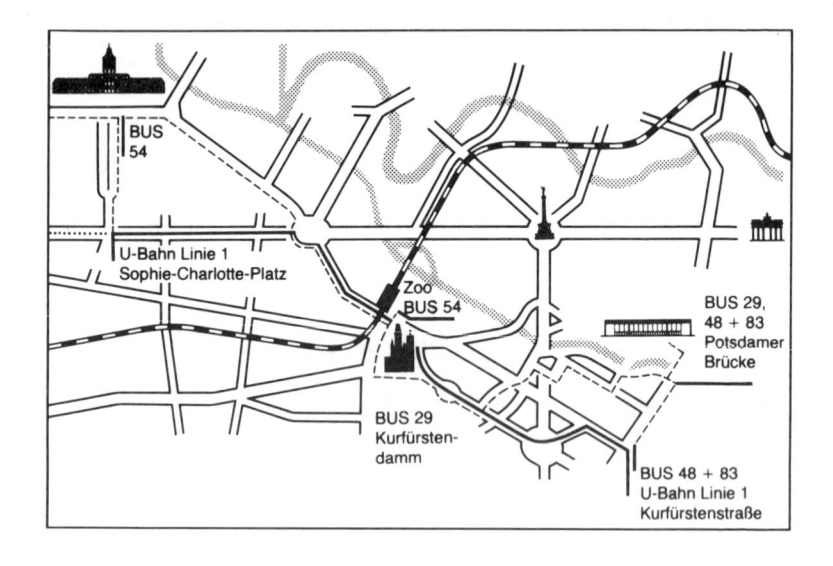

Verkehrsverbindungen

Bus 54 gegenüber dem Schloß
bis Bahnhof Zoo, kurzer Fußweg
zum Kurfürstendamm, umsteigen
in den Bus 29 bis Potsdamer Brücke

oder Fußweg bis U-Bahnhof
Sophie-Charlotte-Platz, Linie 1
bis U-Bahnhof Kurfürstenstraße,
umsteigen in den Bus 48 oder 83
bis Potsdamer Brücke.

READING
11 Two letters

Because you know some German, the manageress of your local tourist information centre has asked you to help her with two letters in German which she has received. Read the letters and give the information requested below in English.

Matthias Rohrmann
Drususstr. 18
6472 Altenstadt

Altenstadt, 31. 10. 88

Das Fundbüro
Verkehrsamt,
Manchester

Betr.: Verlorener Fotoapparat

Sehr geehrte Damen und Herren,

vor kurzem habe ich an einer Ihrer Bustouren teilgenommen. Es war die Fahrt vom 14. 10. 8 zum Seen-Gebiet. Bei dieser Tour habe ich, wie ich Ihrer Reiseleiterin Frl. Smith schon mitgeteilt habe, meinen Fotoapparat verloren. Leider habe ich ich seit dieser Zeit keine weitere Nachricht von Ihnen erhalten. Deshalb möchte ich jetzt nochmals anfragen ob mein Fotoapparat gefunden wurde.
Schon im voraus vielen Dank für Ihre Bemühungen.

Mit freundlichen Grüßen.

Matthias Rohrmann

Letter 1

1 What contact has Matthias already had with the town? (2)
2 Explain his reason for writing on this occasion.
3 To which department did Matthias send his letter?
4 What has Miss Smith to do with the matter?
5 Why might we sympathise with Matthias when he sounds peeved?

Answers: 1 He went on a coach-trip from there to the Lake District. 2 He wants news of his lost camera. 3 The lost property office. 4 Matthias had reported the loss to her. 5 He might have expected at least a reply from the office by now.

> Abs. Jörg Göllner Altenstadt, den 31.10.1985
> Römerstr. 6
> 6472 Altenstadt 1
>
> An das
> Informationsamt Birmingham
>
> Sehr geehrte Damen und Herren!
>
> Am 12.12.1985 spielt unsere Schulkapelle in der Birmingham Grammar School anläßlich der 400-Jahr-Feier der Schule.
> Wir möchten Sie bitten, uns bei der Quartier-Beschaffung behilflich zu sein.
> Wir sind 20 Jungen und Mädchen im Alter von 14-19 Jahren (7 Mädchen und 13 Jungen).
> Wir müßten allerdings sicher sein, daß die Schülerinnen und Schüler gut untergebracht und betreut werden.
>
> Wenn Sie uns damit helfen könnten, wären wir Ihnen außerordentlich dankbar.
>
> mit freundlichen Grüßen
> Jörg Jölle
> (Jörg Göllner)
>
> P.S. Zwei Freikarten für das Konzert habe ich diesem Brief beigelegt.

Letter 2

1 What is to happen on December 12th? (2)
2 Why has Jörg written to this office?
3 Give full details of the group. (3)
4 Why does Jörg sound a little concerned?
5 What does the P.S. tell us?

Answers: 1 The Altenstadt school band will play at Birmingham Grammar school, to celebrate its 400th anniversary. 2 To see if they can help to obtain accommodation for the band. 3 There are 20 young people; aged 14–19; seven young ladies, seven young men (3). 4 It is important to make sure that they are well looked-after. 5 Jörg has enclosed two complimentary tickets for the concert.

READING
12 Television programmes

Aufgabe Look at the television page from today's newspaper below:
1 Find the times of all today's sports programmes on the two channels.
2 Give the times of the news and news-magazine programmes on Channel 1.
3 Which programmes are you likely to watch if you are interested in Pop?
4 When and on which channel do you get the National Lottery news?
5 You like comedy films. Which programme are you likely to watch?
6 There is a choice of westerns. Find them both.

Tips!

1 *Nachrichten/Tagesschau* are the usual titles which indicate a news programme. *Das Zweite Programm* uses *Heute* instead. *Schau* actually means *a look at*. You also find it in *Sportschau* (a look at the sport).
2 If you are not sure whether a particular programme is a play or a film, see if the information has *Spieldauer* (running-time) at the end. If it has, you know it's a film.
3 If you can't work out whether a programme is a single film or part of a series, look for the word *Folge*, as in *2.Programm, 15.45. 2. Folge* 2nd Part. *Nächste Folge: Freitag* Next part: Friday.

Answers: 1 10.23, 12.00, 13.30, 14.00, 18.05, 22.05, 21.55 (7). 2 10.00, 11.45, 17.30, 18.00, 20.00, 22.05, 1.35 (7). 3 2.Programm at 15.00, 18.20 (2). 4 Channel 1 at 22.00 (=10 pm) (2). 5 1.Programm at 20.15 (1). 6 Programm 1 at 22.20, Programm 2 at 20.15 (2).

1.PROGRAMM

Gemeinsames Vormittagsprogramm
10.00 Tagesschau/Tagesthemen 10.23 Die Sport-Reportage (Wdh. vom Vortag) 10.55 Geschichten aus der Heimat (Wdh. vom Donnerstag) 11.40 Pressechau 11.45 Tagesschau

12.00 Sport extra
Leichtathletik-Weltcup
Aufzeichnung aus Canberra
Mehr zu dieser Sendung links
13.30 Zwischen den Sätzen
(BR) Désirée Nosbusch im Gespräch mit Jungprofi Boris Becker
14.00 Sport extra
Tennis-Daviscup-Halbfinale
Bundesrepublik gegen ČSSR:
Doppel – Live aus Frankfurt
Die Spieler werden kurzfristig benannt. Zu rechnen ist mit Boris Becker. Voraussichtlicher Partner: Andreas Maurer

2.PROGRAMM

11.00 Programmvorschau
11.30 Chemie
Erste von 13 Wiederhalungen: „Eine schöne Verwandtschaft: Die Alkalimentalle" – Einführung in den Aufbau des Periodensystems (jeweils samstags 11.30 Uhr) – (**Wdh.** v. 74) Begleitbücher zur Serie (Verlagsgellschaft Schulfernsehen, Köln) sind im Buchhandel erhältlich
12.00 Nachbarn in Europa
Berichte und Musik 12.00 Portugal 12.40 Italien 13.20 Türkei
14.00 Diese Woche
14.20 Damals – Vor vierzig Jahren:
Neuaufbau der Gewerkschaften

1.PROGRAMM

16.45 Unsere kleine Farm
Heute: „Lauras Eifersucht"
17.30 Regionalprogramm
Siehe unten
18.00 Tagesschau
18.05 Die Sportschau
Mehr zu Sendung links

Regionalprogramm
HR, Frankfurt 17.30 Zentrale Bangkok **19.00** Sport-Stenogramm **19.05** Sandmännchen **19.20** Hessenschau
WDR, Köln 17.30 Hier und Heute unterwegs **19.00** Markt **19.25** Blam
SDR/SWF, Stuttgart/Baden-Baden 17.30 Zentrale Bangkok **19.00** Sandmännchen: Ein Jahr mit Melanie **19.15** Abendschauen
BR, München 17.30 Zwischen Spessart und Karwendel **19.00** Sanstagsclub der Abendschau **19.40** Abendschau/Sport
SR, Saarbrücken 17.30 Zentrale Bangkok? **19.00** Sandmännchen **19.10** Daten der Woche **19.25** Aktueller Bericht

19.58 Heute im Ersten
20.00 Tagesschau
20.15 Der Komödienstadel
(BR) „Der Onkel Pepi" – Live aus der Nürnberger Frankenhalle
Es spielen: Franzi (Katharina de Bruyn), Pepi (Gerd Fitz), Keiler (Franz Hanfstingl), Sepp (Hans Kraus), Evi (Gabriele Grund), Egon (Rolf Castell) und andere
Mehr zu dieser Sendung links
(Wdh. 12. Oktober, 10.35 Uhr)
22.00 Lottozahlen – 40. Ziehung

						+	

Spiel 77

22.05 Tagesschau/Sport
Danach: Des Wort zum Sonntag
22.20 Vergeltung ohne Gnade
US-Western aus dem Jahre 1960 Es spielen: Barrett (Alan Ladd), Dan (Don Murray), Julie (Dolores Michaels), Ivers (Dan O'Herlihy) u.a. – Regie: James B. Clark Mehr zu dieser Sendung links
23.30 Mission Galactica:
Angriff der Zylonen
US-Science-fiction-Film, 1979
Regie: Vince Edwards/Christian Nyby II – (Wdh. von 1981)
Mehr zu dieser Sendung links
1.35 Tagesschau
1.40 Nachtgedanken
Sendeschluß ca. 1.45 Uhr

2.PROGRAMM

14.30 Die einzige Geschichte
Ein Bericht über die Schriftstellerin Friederike Roth
Von Norbert Beilharz – Die Autorin, geboren 1948, erheilt 1983 für ihr „Buch des Lebens" den Ingeborg-Bachmann-Preis
15.00 Jeder braucht Musik
(stereo) Junge Künstler musizieren
Mit Prof. Hermann Rauhe
Werke von Carl Orff, Orlando di Lasso, Max Reger, Leopold Mozart, Richard Strauss u. a.
15.45 Wallenstein
2. Folge: „Die großen Geschäfte" – (Wdh. v. 78) Es spielen: Wallenstein (Rolf Boysen), Ferdinand II. (Romuald Pekny), Maximilian I. (Werner Kreindl), Tilly (E. F. Fürbringer), Eggenberg (Karl Schwetter), Collalto (Karl Walter Diess), Lamormaini (Hans Caninenberg), Harrach (Franz Stoss), Isabella (Erika Deutinger), Thurn (Wolfgang Preiss), de Witte (Stephan Orlac), Magni (K. M. Vogler) u. a.
Mehr zu dieser Sendung rechts
Nächste Folge: Freitag, 14.55
17.17 Danke schön – Mit den Gewinnern vom Großen Preis
17.25 Heute
17.30 Länderspiegel
18.20 Solid Gold
US-Tophits mit Tommi Ohrner
17.57 ZDF – Ihr Programm
19.00 Heute
19.30 Na, sowas!
(stereo) Gäste bei Thomas Gottschalk
Mehr zu dieser Sendung rechts
20.15 Man nannte ihn Hombre
US-Western von 1966 mit Paul Newman – Regie: Martin Ritt („Der Spion, der aus der Kälte kam") – (Wdh. von 1983)
Mehr zu dieser Sendung rechts
21.50 Heute
21.55 Das aktuelle Sport-Studio
Mit Doris Papperitz
Gewinnzahlen   VPS 23.09
23.10 Mein Leben ist der Rhythmus
(SW)
US-Spielfilm von 1958 mit Elvis Presley – Regie: Michael Curtiz Es spielen: Danny (Elvis Presley), Ronnie (Carolyn Jones), Maxie (Walter Matthau), Nellie (Dolores Hart), Pop (Dean Jagger) u. a. – Buch: Harold Robbins
Mehr zu dieser Sendung rechts
1.00 Heute
Sendeschluß ca. 1.05 Uhr

READING
13 Newspaper reports

Steffi und Boris erneut Turniersieger

Zeigte in Brighton einen großen Kampf: Steffi Graf. Bild: dpa

Brighton/Tokio (dpa). Zweifacher Triumph für das deutsche Tennis: In Brighton gewann die 17jährige Heidelbergerin Steffi Graf zunächst sowohl das Finale im Einzel mit 6:3, 6:3 gegen die Schwedin Catarina Lindqvist als auch an der Seite der Tschechoslowakin Helena Sukova das Doppel mit 6:4, 6:4 gegen Bettina Scheuer-Larsen/Cathy Tanvier (Dänemark/Frankreich). – Boris Becker (Leimen) gewann das Tennis-Turnier von Tokio durch einen 7:6, 6:1-Sieg über den Schweden Stefan Edberg. Becker hatte im Halbfinale den Amerikaner Jimmy Connors bezwungen.

58 *Newspaper reports*

Aufgabe   Look at the article on page 57, and answer the following questions:

1   What are we told by the title of this short article?
3   Why is Brighton a double triumph?
3   Who won two titles and what were they? (2)
4   What did Boris Becker win on this occasion?
5   Name three of the four players in the men's semi-finals at Tokyo. (3)

tips!   In match reports, look first for the following:

1   *Schlüsselwörter:*
    gewinnen win;   *der Kampf* battle, struggle;   *das Finale* the final;   *gegen* against;   *das Doppel* doubles;   *das Turnier* tournament;   *der Sieg* victory; *das Halbfinale* semi-final;   *das Einzelspiel* singles; *das Endspiel* final (game);   *die Mannschaft* team;   *der Mitglied* member;   *die Meisterschaft* championship.

    Learn this vocabulary by heart, since a sports item is likely to occur in either the Listening or the Reading paper and, more important, you may well want or need to talk about sport in any German-speaking country you visit.

2   Look to see who the person is in the sports photograph, and try to work out the expression on his or her face. This will often help you to understand the headline and/or how the person photographed has done.

14 Agony Uncle

Aufgabe Read the passage on page 60, then answer the questions in English, giving all the necessary information.

1 Why is this reader afraid of being laughed at?
2 Explain her problem.
3 Why precisely does she feel like a *Gartenzwerg*?
4 What makes her feel particularly unhappy? (2)
5 What advice does she normally get? (3)
6 Why do her dreams depress her?
7 What precise information does she require from the magazine doctor?

Answers: 1 Because this is what her parents and brothers and sisters do. 2 She thinks she is much too small, only 5' 2". 3 Her friends are all almost a head bigger than her. 4 She thinks boys will not be interested in her, and she will not find a husband. 5 That's life; she must make the best of it; she'll surely find a husband. 6 In her dreams, the men are so tall that she hardly comes up to their chest. 7 How she can be made a few centimetres taller.

Bitte lachen Sie mich nicht aus, wie das meine Eltern und Geschwister tun. Ich (15) leide grausam darunter, viel zu klein zu sein. Ich bin nur 1,54 m groß, besser gesagt klein. Gegenüber meinen Freundinnen, die alle bis zu einen Kopf größer sind als ich, komme ich mir vor wie ein Gertenzwerg. Ich bin so unglücklich über meinen Zwergenwuchs. Wie soll sich jemals ein Junge für mich interessieren, wie soll ich jemals einen Mann finden. Geben Sie mir nur nicht den Allerweltsrat, das sei nun einmal so, ich müsse mich damit abfinden, und auch als kleine Frau würde ich mit sicherheit einen Mann bekommen. Ich kann diesen Quatsch schon nicht mehr ertragen. Die Männer, von denen ich träume, sind so riesengroß, daß sie sich mit mir an ihrer Seite nur lächerlich machen würden. Wie sieht das aus, eine Frau, die ihrem Mann höchstens bis zur Brust reicht?. Nein, ich will um jeden Preis ein paar Zentimeter größer werden. Bitte sagen Sie mir, wie ich das erreichen kann.

Dr. Helmut Demel, Sexualmediziner

● *Viele schöne Frauen, die Männerherzen höher schlagen lassen, sind auch nicht viel größer als Du, Zum Bei-spiel Liz Taylor, Sydne Rome, Joan Collins. Und eine Befragung unter bekannten Mädchenfotografen für Herrenmagazine ergab, daß ihre beliebtensten Models alle um 1,60 m groß sind. Wichtig ist doch nur, daß die Proportionen stimmen. Mach Dich so hübsch wie möglich und Dir keine Sorgen mehr. Gerade große Männer mögen kleine Frauen oft besonders gern, weil da ihr „Beschützerinstinkt" durchbricht.*

SPEAKING

The work in this skill is divided into three sections: 1 role-play, 2 general conversation, and 3 situation narrative.

In Section 1 (and indeed, in all of the speaking work), if you have the cassette, *listen* to the recorded material several times *before* you start speaking.

If you find your Board requires you to work on Picture Narrative for your Oral Examination, turn to pp. 114–119 in the Writing Section. (Again, if you have the cassette, listen to the narratives before attempting to recount them.)

General hints

1 Wherever possible, avoid giving simple *ja* or *nein* answers to the questions you are asked. Try, instead, to give full statements (which need not be full sentences) for answers.

2 Try to give more information than the absolute minimum, e.g.
   Examiner: Wo wohnen Sie denn?
   You: Ich wohne in Axbridge. + Das ist eine kleine Stadt nicht so weit von hier. + Ich wohne gern da.

3 *Sounding natural:* Oral tests can be very drab for both you and the examiner if you limit yourself to just answering the questions, so don't be afraid to express your feelings in what you are saying. If, for example, the examiner has hit upon a topic you are keen on, sound *enthusiastic* when you talk. Similarly, don't be afraid to be a little humorous from time to time, as long as you don't overdo it.

4 Try to avoid using bald statements all the time. If you think of the way you speak English, you will realise that you frequently add little words and phrases to give your language a natural flow, e.g.: *Well/Right/Me, I . . . /You see/You know/Let's say . . .*

Look at the following list of similar German expressions and work out which *statement-starters* you can introduce into your German, without its sounding false:

Gut . . .	*Well* . . .	Alles klar!	*Fine!*
Na ja . . .	*Well* . . .	Ja, ja, ja!	*Yes, indeed!*
Einverstanden . . .	*Okay* . . .	Nein, nein, nein!	*No, indeed!*
Ich aber . . .	*Me, I* . . .	Ach, ja . . .	*Oh yes* . . .
Wissen Sie . . .	*You know* . . .	Ach, nein . . .	*Oh no* . . .
Sagen wir . . .	*Let's say* . . .	Pfui . . .	*Ugh* . . .
Na, und!	*So what!*	Auf keinem Fall!	*Not at all!*

5 Ask one or two questions of the examiner yourself, if a suitable occasion presents itself. It would not, for example, be out of place to ask him or her what parts of Germany he or she knew well and what he or she liked about the country.

SPEAKING
Role-play 1

Practice each role-play yourself, before listening to or checking the sample version below. Remember that there are many different ways of saying things, besides those given in the sample.

Saying Goodbye
Imagine you are about to return home after a holiday in a German-speaking country and that you are saying goodbye to someone. Your teacher (friend, etc) will take the part of this other person.

Basic level
1 Explain that you have come to say goodbye.
2 Say you intend to leave tomorrow.
3 Add that you hope to come back another time.
4 Ask if the person is coming to the station with you.

Higher level
5 Ask if the person wishes to continue with the school exchange.
6 Ask if the whole family would like to come and stay with you at Easter.

Freund(in): Hallo! Ist heute dein letzter Tag hier?
Ich: Eben. Ich komme, um auf Wiedersehen zu sagen.
Freund(in): Und wann fährst du denn ab?
Ich: Ich glaube, morgen früh gegen elf Uhr.
Freund(in): Ach, so.
Ich: Hoffentlich werde ich nächstes Jahr zurückkommen.
Freund(in): Hoffen wir das.
Ich: Möchtest du morgen mit mir zum Bahnhof gehen?
Freund(in): Ohne weiteres.

Ich: Und möchtest du nächstes Jahr am Schulaustausch teilnehmen?
Freundin: Ja, sicher.
Ich: Meine Eltern möchten deine ganze Familie einladen, nächste Ostern bei uns zu verbringen.
Freud(in): Das ist ja unheimlich nett! Ich frage meine Eltern!

SPEAKING
Role-play 2

At the customs
You are going through the customs, having just arrived in a German-speaking country. Your teacher/partner will take the part of the customs officer.

Basic level
1 State what nationality you are.
2 Ask if the officer wishes to see your passport.
3 Tell her/him that you have a rucksack and a sports bag.
4 Say that you have a Japanese camera in your rucksack.

Higher level
5 Tell the officer that you have 200 Marks in 10 Mark notes, plus £50 in traveller's cheques.
6 Ask if it is alright for you to bring in 100 ml of perfume, as you are 17 years old.

Zollbeamter/-beamtin: Sind Sie denn Amerikaner(in)?
Ich: Nein, ich komme aus England (Irland, Schottland, Wales). Wollen Sie meinen Paß sehen?
Beamter/Beamtin: Nein, danke . . . . Sagen Sie mir, was für Gepäck haben Sie?
Ich: Ich habe diesen Rucksack und die Sporttasche da.
Beamter/Beamtin: Haben Sie Wertgegenstände drinnen?
Ich: Ja, ja. Einen japanischen Fotoapparat hier im Rucksack.

Beamter/Beamtin: Haben Sie auch genug Geld für Ihren Aufenthalt?
Ich: Ich glaube, ja. Zweihundert Mark in Zehnmark-Scheinen, plus fünfzig Pfund in Reiseschecks.
Beamter/Beamtin: Gut, gut. Und haben Sie etwas zu verzollen?
Ich: Ich habe hundert Gramm Parfüm als Geschenk für die Familie. Geht das? Ich bin siebzehn Jahre alt.
Beamter/Beamtin: Ach, ja. Sie können gehen. Schöne Ferien!
Ich: Vielen Dank.

SPEAKING
Role-play 3

At a camp-site
You have just arrived at a camp-site. Your teacher/partner will play the site attendant.

Basic level
1 Ask if there is room for a caravan plus a tent for four.
2 Ask if there is electricity laid on.
3 Say you would prefer to be near the beach.
4 Ask if there is a camp shop.

Higher level
5 Ask if there is a reduction for students, and say you have your student card with you.
6 Ask where the gas-bottle depot is, and whether the shower-block has shaver-sockets.

Leiter(in): Guten Abend. Was kann ich für Sie tun?
Ich: Haben Sie noch Platz? Wir haben einen Wohnwagen und ein Vierpersonenzelt!
Leiter(in): Ja, ich glaube, wir haben Platz.
Ich: Gibt es auch Strom für den Wohnwagen?
Leiter(in): Ja, die Steckdosen sind neben Ihrem Wagenplatz. Das ist ganz normal. Sie stehen neben dem Wald.
Ich: Haben Sie denn nichts am Strand?
Leiter(in): Tut mir leid, gar nichts da. Sie kommen zu spät.
Ich: Macht nichts. Haben Sie hier ein Campinggeschäft?
Leiter(in): Natürlich. Unser Campingshop ist nicht so weit von Ihrem Platz.

Ich: Gibt es Studentenmäßigungen? Ich habe meinen Ausweis mit.
Leiter(in): Leider gibt es keine Sonderpreise hier während der Hochsaison.
Ich: Bitte, wo kann ich die Gasflaschen finden und ... ach, ja ... gibt es Steckdosen im Waschraum?
Leiter(in): Die Gasflaschen sind draußen in der Hütte vor der Tür, und ja, die Steckdosen sind im Waschraum.
Ich: Schönen Dank.

SPEAKING
Role-play 4

At a garage
You have called into a garage to have your car looked at. Your partner will play the garage mechanic.

Basic level
1. Ask if (s)he will check your car.
2. Say the engine is not working well.
3. Ask to have your brakes checked, too.
4. Say the oil needs checking.

Higher level
5. Ask if the engine problem is because you used 2 Star instead of 4 Star.
6. Tell the attendant you need to phone and ask for the STD code for Cologne.

Mechaniker(in): Guten Tag. Was kann ich für Sie tun?
Ich: Könnten Sie mir den Wagen prüfen?
Mechaniker(in): Jawohl. Wo fehlt's?
Ich: Im Motor. Er läuft nicht gut.
Mechaniker(in): Nanu, ich werde gucken.
Ich: Könnten Sie auch die Bremsen prüfen?
Mechaniker(in) Ja, das kann ich machen.
Ich: Ich glaube, ich habe auch Probleme mit dem Öl. Bitte, würden. Sie da auch nachsehen.
Mechaniker(in): Wird gemacht.

Ich: Ich habe Normal statt Super gebraucht. Könnte das das Motorproblem sein?
Mechaniker(in): Unwahrscheinlich ... Wir werden es gleich wissen.
Ich: Ich muß unbedingt Köln anrufen. Kennen Sie bitte die Vorwahl?
Mechaniker(in): Für Köln wählen sie zwo, zwo, eins.

SPEAKING
Role-play 5

Asking your way
You need to ask your way in a town which is new to you. Your partner will play the passer-by.

Basic level
1 Ask for directions to the swimming baths.
2 Say you have a van, but would prefer to walk, if it is not too far away.
3 Ask if there is a cafe at the baths.
4 Ask if there is a separate pool for young children.

Higher level
5 Ask where you can park your van.
6 Ask if you need a parking disc.

Ich: Entschuldigen Sie, wie komme ich am besten zum Freibad?
Passant(in): Sind Sie zu Fuß oder mit dem Wagen?
Ich: Ich habe einen Lieferwagen, aber ich gehe lieber zu Fuß, wenn es nicht so weit ist.
Passant(in): Sie gehen immer geradeaus bis zu einer Brücke. Sie nehmen die erste Straße links nach der Brücke. Das Freibad ist gleich rechts.
Ich: Danke schön. Gibt's ein Café im Freibad?
Passat(in): Ja, sicher, sogar zwei.
Ich: Gibt es da auch ein Kinderbecken?
Passant(in): Ja, klar. Mein kleiner Neffe geht dahin.

Ich: Bitte, wo kann ich hier meinen Lieferwagen parken?
Passant(in): Um die Ecke da.
Ich: Und brauche ich eine Parkscheibe?
Passant(in): Normalerweise, ja, aber nicht zu dieser Zeit.
Ich: Danke vielmals.
Passant(in): Gern geschehen.

SPEAKING
Role-play 6

Shopping
You are buying a present in a souvenir shop. Your partner will play the salesperson.

Basic level
1 Ask how much the T-shirt you are holding costs.
2 Ask if the one with the motif is the same price.
3 Ask if they have this second T-shirt in size 38.
4 Say that you'll take both T-shirts.

Higher level
5 Ask if the assistant will wrap the T-shirts up as a present.
6 Say politely that (s)he has put the bill in the parcel.

Verkäufer(in): Ja, bitte schön?
Ich: Bitte, wieviel kostet dieses T-shirt hier?
Verkäufer(in): 15 Mark. Das ist 20 Prozent weniger als letzte Woche.
Ich: Und dieses mit dem Badge; ist das derselbe Preis?
Verkäufer(in): Ja, ja. Beide sind gleich.
Ich: Haben Sie dieses mit dem Badge in Größe 38?
Verkäufer(in): Ja, hier, bitte schön.
Ich: Gut. Dann nehme ich die zwei T-shirts.

Ich: Die T-shirts sind ein Geschenk. Könnten Sie mir bitte ein kleines Päckchen machen?
Verkäufer(in): Ja, gerne . . .
Ich: Es tut mir leid, aber Sie haben die Quittung eingepackt.
Verkäufer(in): Ach, ja, es tut mir sehr leid.
Ich: Macht nichts!

SPEAKING
Role-play 7

At the post office
You are in a German post office. Your partner will play the counter-clerk.

Basic level
1 Ask how much it costs to send a postcard and a letter to your home country.
2 Ask for four stamps for cards, and two for letters.
3 Say you would also like to send a telegram.
4 Ask how much it costs per word.

Higher level
5 Ask if the address is counted in the words.
6 Ask how long the telegram will take to arrive.

Beamter/in: Ja, bitte?
Ich: Wieviel kosten eine Ansichtskarte und ein Brief nach England?
Beamter/in: 70 Pfennig und eine Mark.
Ich: Auf diesen Fall, 4 zu 70 und 2 zu eine Mark, bitte.
Beamter/in: Bitte schön.
Ich: Ich möchte auch ein Telegramm nach England schicken.
Beamter/in: Jetzt können Sie nur privat eins schicken. Hier ist ein Formular.
Ich: Und wieviel kostet das je Wort, bitte?
Beamter/in: Knapp eine Mark das Wort.

Ich: Muß ich auch die Adresse zahlen?
Beamter/in: Ja, das müssen Sie.
Ich: Ja, ja! Und wie lange dauert es?
Beamter/in: Morgen wird es da sein.
Ich: Schon gut.

SPEAKING
Role-play 8

Public transport – the railway station
You are enquiring about trains at the station booking-office. Your partner will play the booking clerk.

Basic level
1 Ask what trains there are for Bonn in the evening.
2 Say which is direct.
3 Say you would like a second-class return.
4 Say you would like to reserve a seat.

Higher level
5 Find out if there is a sleeper service.
6 Ask if it is a high-speed train.

Beamter/Beamtin: Wie kann ich Ihnen helfen?
Ich: Bitte, welche Züge fahren heute abend nach Bonn?
Beamter/Beamtin: 18 Uhr 25, 19 Uhr 25 und so weiter bis 23 Uhr 25.
Ich: Danke. Und fahren sie alle direkt?
Beamter/Beamtin: Keine Sorge! Alle fahren direkt. Sie brauchen nicht umzusteigen!
Ich: Danke vielmals... Einmal nach Bonn, bitte... zweite Klasse, hin und zurück.
Beamter/Beamtin: 390 Mark, bitte. Bis 20 Uhr 25 sind die Züge normalerweise voll besetzt.
Ich: Dann möchte ich einen Platz reservieren.
Beamter/Beamtin: Ja, freilich.

Ich: Gibt es einen Schlafwagen oder ein Liegewagen?
Beamter/Beamtin: Nur ab 22 Uhr 25.
Ich: Und ist mein Zug ein Schnellzug?
Beamter/Beamtin: Ja, ja. Er ist ein TEE!

SPEAKING
Role-play 9

Public transport – the underground
You are enquiring about tube trains at the ticket office. Your partner will play the clerk.

Basic level
1 Ask which line you have to take for the *Gedächtniskirche*.
2 Ask whether you have to change.
3 Ask how much a single ticket and a saver-strip cost.
4 Ask if there are any reductions for students.

Higher level
5 Enquire whether you can use the tickets on the bus routes as well.
6 Request a plan of the *U-bahn* and any other publicity material on the West Berlin transport system.

Ich: Welche Linie brauche ich für die Gedächtniskirche, bitte?
Beamter/Beamtin: Gucken Sie mal . . . die hier.
Ich: Muß ich umsteigen?
Beamter/Beamtin: Ist nicht nötig. Gucken Sie noch mal. Ist ja direkt.
Ich: Wieviel kostet ein Fahrschein und auch eine Mehrfahrtskarte?
Beamter/Beamtin: Der Fahrschein, eine Mark fünfzig. Die Mehrfahrtskarte, zwölf Mark für zehn Fahrten.
Ich: Ich nehme die Mehrfahrtskarte, bitte. Gibt es auch Studentenmäßigungen?
Beamter/Beamtin: Nicht für Mehrfahrtskarten!

Ich: Kann ich die Karte auch für Busreisen gebrauchen?
Beamter/Beamtin: Für bestimmte Linien, ja. Besser nachsehen.
Ich: Darf ich bitte eine U-bahnkarte haben? Und auch andere Informationen über das Berliner Verkehrsnetz?
Beamter/Beamtin: Ja, bitte schön.

SPEAKING
Role-play 10

At a restaurant
You are ordering a meal at a restaurant. Your partner will play the waiter/waitress.

Basic level
1 Order roast chicken, chips and salad.
2 Ask what white wine there is.
3 Ask for a carafe of sweet white wine.
4 Draw attention to the fact that you do not have a knife and fork.

Higher level
5 Complain that the chicken has not been cooked for long enough.

Kellner(in): Was darf es sein?
Ich: Ich esse gern ein Brathähnchen mit Pommes Frites und Salat.
Kellner(in): Gut. Und was möchten Sie dazu trinken?
Ich: Was für Weißwein haben Sie?
Kellner(in): Piesporter, Liebfraumilch, Niersteiner, Gewürztraminer, Rheinhessen, und so weiter.
Ich: Würden Sie mir bitte eine Karaffe lieblichen Weißwein bringen.
Kellner(in): Ja, sicher.
Ich: Bitte, es tut mir leid ... ich habe keine Gabel und kein Messer.
Kellner(in): Entschuldigung. Ich bringe sie Ihnen sofort.

Ich: Verzeihung, aber das Hähnchen ist nicht gar.
Kellner(in): Tatsächlich? Wenn sie möchten bringen sie ich ein anderes.

SPEAKING
Role-play 11

Reporting lost property
You are reporting the loss of your rucksack to the police. Your partner will play the duty officer.

Basic level
1. Report that you have lost your rucksack.
2. When you are asked what was in it, say there was your purse/wallet and some travellers' cheques.
3. Say you think you lost it in the pedestrian precinct this afternoon.
4. Say you also went to the Information Office for a map.

Higher level
5. Inform the officer that the bag can be identified by a label with your name and address.
6. Say that you are passing through.

Beamter/Beamtin: Was kann ich für Sie tun?
Ich: Ich habe meinen Rücksack verloren.
Beamter/Beamtin: Hatten Sie viel drinnen?
Ich: Meine Geldtasche und einige Reiseschecks!
Beamter/Beamtin: Wissen sie, wo Sie den Rücksack verloren haben?
Ich: Ich glaube, in der Fußgängerzone heute nachmittag.
Beamter/Beamtin: Sind Sie anderswohin gegangen?
Ich: Nein ... doch, doch ... zum Verkehrsamt für einen Stadtplan.

Beamter/Beamtin: Kann man Ihn Sack leicht identifizieren?
Ich: Er hat einen Anhänger mit meiner Anschrift und Adresse.
Beamter/Beamtin: Ihre Adresse hier in der Stadt?
Ich: Nein, ich bin hier auf der Durchreise.

SPEAKING
Role-play 12

Arranging to meet someone
You are arranging to meet a friend. Your partner will play the friend.

Basic level
1 Ask if your friend would like to go out with a group of you this evening.
2 Say you haven't any homework to do.
3 Suggest that you go bowling.
4 Ask if your friend would like to go for a drink after.

Higher level
5 Say you think it's reduced-price night at the bowling rink.
6 Say you can get your friends in cheaply because you know the owner.

Ich: Wollen wir nicht mit der Gruppe heute abend ausgehen?
Freund(in): Hast du keine Hausaufgaben auf?
Ich: Heute nicht . . . gar keine!
Freund(in): Ich auch nicht.
Ich: Wir könnten alle zur Kegelbahn gehen, nicht wahr?
Freund(in): Ja, ja. Eine gute Idee!
Ich: Spater könnten wir etwas zusammen trinken?
Freund(in): Ja, warum nicht!

Ich: Ich glaube, heute ist Halb-Preis-Abend bei der Kegelbahn!
Freund(in): Um so besser!
Ich: Wenn nicht, können wir es auch billiger haben, denn der Eigentümer ist ein Freund von mir.

SPEAKING
Role-play 13

At the doctor's
You are feeling poorly, and pay a visit to the doctor's. Your partner will play the doctor.

Basic level
1 Say you feel ill.
2 Say you have a headache and a stomach-ache.
3 Say you are also being sick.
4 Tell the doctor you need some medicine.

Higher level
5 Say that your temperature is three degrees above normal.
6 Complain that you are shivering all the time.

Arzt/Ärztin: Wo fehlt's?
Ich: Es geht mir schlecht.
Arzt/Ärztin: Haben Sie Schmerzen oder was?
Ich: Ich habe Kopf- und Magenschmerzen.
Arzt/Ärztin: Kopf- und Magenschmerzen, nanu . . .
Ich: Ich übergebe mich auch dann und wann.
Arzt/Ärztin: Ich mache eine kleine Untersuchung.
Ich: Ich brauche keine Untersuchung, nur Medizin.
Arzt/Ärztin: Wir werden sehen.

Ich: Meine Temperatur ist drei Grad höher als normal.
Arzt/Ärztin: Das kann ich sehen!
Ich: Und ich zittere die ganze Zeit.
Arzt/Ärztin: Ist klar . . . Sie haben eine Grippe. Ich gebe Ihnen eine Medizin, aber Sie müssen sowieso zu Bett gehen!

SPEAKING
Role-play 14

At the cinema
You are at the cash-desk in a German cinema. Your partner will play the cashier.

Basic level
1 Ask what time the show starts.
2 Ask if the programme is continuous.
3 Enquire whether the film has already begun.
4 Ask what time the performance ends.

Higher level
5 Ask if there are any shorts to go with the main film.
6 Ask if there are reduced prices for students.

Kassierer(in): Bitte schön?
Ich: Bitte, wann fängt die Vorstellung an?
Kassierer(in): Um 7 Uhr 45.
Ich: Ist das ein durchgehender Einlaß?
Kassierer(in): Nein, es gibt nur eine Vorstellung.
Ich: Hat der Film schon angefangen?
Kassierer(in): Noch nicht. Sie kommen zur rechten Zeit. Sie haben fünf Minuten.
Ich: Und wann endet der Film?
Kassierer(in): Um 10 Uhr 25.

Ich: Kommen auch Kurzspielfilme dazu?
Kassierer(in): Nein, Sie haben gar nichts versäumt.
Ich: Gibt es auch Sonderpreise für Studenten?
Kassierer(in): Für diesen Film ja, wenn Sie Ihren Ausweis bei sich haben.

SPEAKING
Role-play 15

Ordering a snack
You are at a cafe. Your partner will play the waiter/waitress.

Basic level
1 Ask for the menu.
2 Order two different soft drinks – one for your friend and one for yourself.
3 Order one cheese on toast and one hamburger.
4 Ask for two slices of raspberry tart.

Higher level
5 Say the bill is not correct.
6 Ask to see the manager(ess).

Kellner(in): Was kann ich Ihnen bringen?
Ich: Ich möchte die Speisekarte, bitte.
Kellner(in): Bitte schön.
Ich: Eine Cola für mich und eine Fanta für meinen Freund, bitte.
Kellner(in): Und was möchten Sie denn essen?
Ich: Eine überbackene Käseschnitte und einen Hamburger, bitte.
Kellner(in): Wird gemacht!
Ich: Wir hätten auch Lust auf ein Stück Himbeertorte.
Kellner(in): Und zweimal Himbeertorte.

Ich: Herr Ober!/Fräulein!
Kellner(in): Sie wünschen noch etwas?
Ich: Es tut mir leid, aber es ist ein Fehler in der Rechnung ...
Kellner(in): Nein, 18 Mark 40 ... das stimmt ... ist ja alles in Ordnung.
Ich: Überhaupt nicht! Das ist drei Mark zuviel. Kann ich mit dem Geschäftsführer sprechen?
Kellner(in): Wie Sie möchten.

SPEAKING
Role-play 16

At the service station
You have stopped at a service station for petrol. Your partner will play the attendant.

Basic level
1 Ask for 20 litres of two-star.
2 Change your mind and ask the attendant to fill the tank.
3 Ask him/her to clean the windscreen.
4 Ask if they have a map of the area.

Higher level
5 Ask where the next motorway exit is.
6 Ask if there is a hotel near that exit.

Tankwart/Tankwärtin: Was soll es sein?
Ich: Zwanzig Liter Normal, bitte.
Tankwart/Tankwärtin: Zwanzig Liter Normal.
Ich: Nein . . . besser . . . volltanken . . . ?
Tankwart/Tankwärtin: Gern geschehen!
Ich: Würden Sie mir bitte auch die Scheibe putzen?
Tankwart/Tankwärtin: Ja, freilich . . . Sonst etwas?
Ich: Haben Sie bitte eine Karte der Gegend?
Tankwart/Tankwärtin: Die haben wir sicher drinnen.

Ich: Wo finde ich die nächste Ausfahrt, bitte?
Tankwart/Tankwärtin: Etwa 10 Kilometer weiter, Richtung Bonn-Köln.
Danke schön. Gibt es ein Hotel neben der Ausfahrt?
Tankwart/Tankwärtin: Ein Hotel, nein . . . aber ein Motel, ja.
Ich: Recht schönen Dank!

SPEAKING
General conversation

Work through these questions frequently, until the answers become automatic. To help yourself, think of it as a matter of pride to speak as well as you can in your Oral, because perhaps the main reason we learn a language in the first place is to be able to speak.

There are several things you can do to give yourself the best chance of doing well in your general conversation:

1 When you are asked a question, try to give as much information as possible. For example, if you are asked where you live, don't just give the name of the town or village. Say something about your house, its address, the street you live in, how near the country you are, whether your home is a bit isolated, how far it is from school, etc.
2 Avoid *ja* and *nein* answers. Always try to give a compete answer.
3 Politeness is also a help. Remember to refer to your examiner as *Herr Davies/Fräulein Jones/Frau Williams* from time to time. Don't do it before or after every sentence, as this becomes rather artificial.
4 Try to start a fair number of your answers with little expressions of agreement/disagreement, etc, such as:
Ja, sicher/Natürlich/Ohne weiteres/Einverstanden/Keineswegs/Durchaus nicht/Wenn nötig/Es ist unwahrscheinlich/Stimmt/Tatsächlich/Wenn ich muß, etc.

Similarly, if you are expressing an opinion, try to lead into it with expressions like:
Für mich . . . /Meinerseits . . . /Für meine Person . . . /Meiner Meinung nach . . . /Ich glaube . . . /Es scheint mir, daß . . . /Ich bin der Ansicht . . .
5 We have talked a lot about your answering questions. When you think of it, this makes for a very one-sided conversation, with the examiner asking all the questions and you doing all the answering! If the examiner asks you to talk about your hobbies, interests, etc, or asks your opinion of something, don't be afraid to ask whether he or she shares the same interests or feelings. Again, don't do this all the time, because that would make the conversation sound false, but you are perfectly within your rights to ask some questions of your examiner. Use questions such as:

Spielen Sie auch (Klavier, Trompete, Posaune, Hockey, Fußball, Rugby, Tennis)?
Interessieren Sie sich auch dafür?
Welche Sportart/Welches Instrument ziehen Sie vor?
Machen Sie auch (Aerobik)?
Waren Sie auch schon in (Stuttgart)?
Haben Sie die Stadt besucht?
Wie hat sie Ihnen gefallen?
Wie ist Ihre Meinung darüber?

Wie stehen Sie dazu?
Haben Sie ... im Fernsehen gesehen?

As long as you don't overdo it, two or three questions asked of the examiner at the right time will quite cheer him or her up, as an examiner's day can be rather boring. Examiners are generally limited to asking questions and do not often have the chance to talk about themselves.

If you have the supplementary cassette or can record the questions yourselves, we suggest you use the tape of the general conversation questions in the following way:

1 Take the questions a section at a time. First, listen to the questions and answers without looking at the written version. (On the cassette, a possible response has been chosen from among the various alternatives given in the written version.)
2 Now listen to the section again, this time with the text in front of you. Look carefully at the written words, to help you over those answers you find difficult.
3 Now start answering the questions. To do this, press the stop/pause button on the tape after each question and give yourself time to answer it. Then listen to the specimen answer after your own.
4 Work through all the sections in this way. Try using different answers from amongst those given, as well as your own.
5 Once you are confident you can begin to give a competent answer for each question, start using the *snowball* method: try to give two or three statements (or more) in answer to as many questions as possible.
6 Play the tape through casually, when you are putting your make-up on/doing the household chores. Play the tape over and over again, until you are completely familiar with it.

1 Informationen zu Ihrer Person und Ihrer Familie
1 **Wie heißen Sie?**
   Ich heiße ...
2 **Wie ist Ihr Familienname?**
   Mein Familienname ist ...
3 **Haben Sie noch einen Vornamen?**
   Ich habe die Vornamen ... und ...
4 **Haben Sie einen Spitznamen?**
   Man nennt mich [„Ginger"] wegen (meiner Haarfarbe).
5 **Hat Ihr Familienname eine deutsche Entsprechung?**
   Ja, er heißt ... auf Deutsch / Nein, es gibt gar keine Entsprechung.
6 **Wieviele Mitglieder hat Ihre Familie?**
   Es sind ... Personen / Wir sind ... in der Familie.
7 **Haben Sie Haustiere?**
   Nein, Haustiere haben wir nicht / Wir haben ... zu Hause.

General conversation

8 **Sind Sie Einzelkind oder haben Sie Geschwister?**
Ich bin der einzige Sohn / die einzige Tochter / Ich habe einen Bruder [2, 3, 4, Brüder] / Ich habe eine Schwester [2, 3, 4 Schwestern] / Ich habe zwei ältere Brüder / Ich habe eine jüngere Schwester.

9 **Wie alt ist Ihre jüngere Schwester?**
Sie ist ... (Jahre alt).

10 **Wie alt sind Ihre älteren Brüder?**
Sie sind [zwei und vier] Jahre älter als ich.

11 **Und wie alt sind Sie denn?**
Ich bin ... (Jahre alt). Ich werde bald [16].

12 **Wie heißt Ihr Vater / Ihre Mutter?**
Er/sie heißt ...

13 **Was ist Ihre Mutter / Ihr Vater von Beruf?**
Sie/er ist als ... tätig.

14 **Wo arbeitet sie/er?**
(Sie/er arbeitet) zu Hause / in der Stadt / im Dorf / auf dem Lande / im Betrieb / im Ausland.

15 **Wann haben Sie Geburtstag?**
Ich habe am [11. Dezember] Geburtstag.

16 **Wie ist Ihr Tierkreiszeichen?**
Ich bin Schütze.

17 **In welchem Jahr sind Sie geboren?**
Ich bin neunzehnhundertzweiundsiebzig geboren.

18 **Wo sind Sie geboren?**
Ich bin in [Leatherhead] geboren.

19 **Wie heißt Ihre Schule?**
Ich besuche [die Park-Gesamtschule in Pontefract].
[das Manchester Gymnasium].
[eine Privatschule, die „High Hopes" heißt].

20 **Und wie weit ist diese Schule?**
So ungefähr drei Kilometer.

21 **Und wie weit von der Schule wohnen Sie denn?**
(Wir wohnen) fünfhundert Meter von der Schule.

General conversation 81

2 Ihr Alltag

1 **Beschreiben Sie mir ein bißchen Ihr Alltagsleben!**
   Es ist nichts Besonderes. Alltag ist Alltag.
2 **Um wieviel Uhr stehen Sie auf?**
   Ich stehe um [halb acht] auf.
3 **Und um wieviel Uhr gehen Sie zu Bett?**
   Es ist sehr unterschiedlich. An Schultagen, sagen wir um halb elf.
4 **Und wann frühstücken Sie?**
   Meistens um Viertel vor acht.
5 **Wann essen Sie denn zu Mittag?**
   In der Schule haben wir die Mittagspause um zwölf Uhr. Ich esse zwischen zwölf und eins.
6 **Und zu Abend?**
   Wir essen gegen sechs Uhr.
7 **Wann verlassen Sie das Haus morgens?**
   Um zehn Minuten nach acht, so ungefähr.
8 **Und wann kommen Sie zurück?**
   Um etwa [4 Uhr 45].
9 **Was machen Sie abends an Wochentagen?**
   Während der Woche mache ich abends meine Hausaufgaben, aber von Zeit zu Zeit gehe ich mit meinen Freunden aus.
10 **Und am Wochenende?**
   Das ist ja ganz anders. Das Wochenende ist mehr entspannt. Ich gehe sehr oft aus. Ich gehe in die Diskos, ins Gasthaus und eventuell ins Kino.
11 **Helfen Sie denn Ihren Eltern bei der Hausarbeit?**
   Ich helfe auch zu Hause. Ich mache die Hausarbeit; zum Beispiel den Abwasch, die Wäsche, die Betten, den Garten und so weiter. Ich besuche auch meine älteren Verwandten
12 **Sie haben gesagt, daß Sie Haustiere haben. Was für Tiere haben Sie?**
   Wir haben einen Hund / 2, 3, 4, Hünde / eine Katze / 2, 3, 4 Katzen / einen Kater / 2, 3, 4 Kater / 1, 2, 3, 4 Meerschweinchen / 1, 2, 3, 4 Hamster / zwei Kanarienvögel.
13 **Was für einen Hund haben Sie?**
   Unser [Hund] ist groß / klein / weder groß noch klein / mittelgroß / hell(grau) / dunkel(braun) / gestreift / zu dick / sehr mager / aggressiv / liebevoll / nervös.

3 Zu Hause

1 Wo wohnen Sie genau?
Ich wohne in Weston-super-Mare / im Stadtzentrum / in der Stadt / in einem Dorf / im Gebirge / auf dem Lande / am Meer / in der Vorstadt / ... Kilometer weit von hier.

2 In was für einem Haus wohnen Sie?
(Ich wohne) in einem Einfamilienhaus / in einem Zweifamilienhaus / in einem Reihenhaus / in einem Wohnblock / in einer Wohnung / in einem Bungalow / in einem Wohnwagen.

3 Beschreiben Sie ein bißchen Ihr Zuhause!
Also, es gibt ... Zimmer insgesamt. Wir haben ... Schlafzimmer / ein Wohnzimmer / eine Küche / ein Badezimmer / eine Dusch / ein Klo / ein Eßzimmer / einen Waschraum.

4 Beschreiben Sie die Möbel!
Es sind ja normale Möbel! Sofa, Sessel, Betten, Tische, Stühle, Vorhänge, Schränke.

5 Was für eine Heizung haben Sie?
Wir haben Zentralheizung / Wir haben Gas / Elektrizität / Öl / Kohle. / Wir heizen unser Haus unsere Wohnung miteinem Heizkessel. / Wir haben traditionelle Kaminfeuer. Wir heizen mit Nachtstrom.

6 Und was sonst noch?
Wir haben Gas/Elektrizität/Leitungswasser/Öl/Kohle. Wir haben eine Badewanne / 1, 2 WCs / eine Dusche / eine Garage / einen Garten / einen Kühlschrank / einen Tiefkühlschrank / ein Telefon / Radio und Fernsehen / ein Video / ein Videobandgerät.

7 Beschreiben Sie kurz Ihre Stadt/Ihr Dorf!
Sie/es ist (ziemlich) groß/klein mit einer Bevölkerung von ... Einwohnern. Sie/es ist ungefähr ... Kilometer weit von ... Es gibt viel / zu tun.

8 Und wo ist Ihr Zuhause?
Im Stadtzentrum / In der Mitte des Dorfes / Am Stadtrand / Im Vorort / Im Grünen / Am Meer / Nicht weit von hier – nur um die Ecke.

General conversation 83

4 Ihre Interessen und Hobbys
(a) Sport
1 **Was sind Ihre Lieblingshobbys? / Was macht Ihnen normalerweise Spaß? / Was machen Sie, wenn Sie nichts zu tun haben?**
Ich treibe Sport / Ich tanze gern / Ich stricke / Ich gehe gern spazieren / Ich gehe oft aus / Ich gehe in die Diskos / Ich gehe ins Kino / Ich spiele Musik / Ich reite / Ich schwimme / Ich fahre rad / Ich lese und sehe gern fern.
2 **Für welche Sportarten interessieren Sie sich?**
Ich spiele Badminton/Cricket/Fußball/Hockey/Tischtennis/Rugby/Squash/Tennis / Ich treibe Leichtathletik / Ich treibe Jogging.
3 **Und wie oft machen Sie denn das?**
... mal pro Woche / Jeden Tag / Sooft ich kann / (es) Kommt darauf an / (Es) Hängt davon ab / Wenn ich keine Arbeit habe / Wenn ich Geld habe / Während der Ferien / Am Wochenende.
4 **Wo machen Sie es?**
Bei mir oder bei Freunden / Im Stadion / Im Sportzentrum / In der (Groß)Stadt / Im Jugendclub / Auf dem Sportplatz / Im Kino / Im Kinoclub.
5 **Und repräsentieren Sie Ihre Schule?**
Nein, noch nicht / Nein, kein Interesse! / Ich spiele nicht oft genug dafür / Ich habe nicht genug Talent dafür! / Ja, ziemlich regelmäßig Ja, seit ... Jahren / Ja, ich repräsentiere auch die Stadt (die Gegend, die Grafschaft) / Ja und nein, ich bin Reservespieler(in).
6 **Ist es teuer, Ihre Sportart zu treiben?**
Es kommt darauf an / Dann und wann, ja, aber im Allgemeinen, nein / Eben, es ist sehr teuer / Mein (Squash)zeug, ja, aber das beiseite muß ich nicht soviel ausgeben / Wenn man das Zeug mietet, ja. Sonst, nicht / Es ist durchaus nicht teuer!
7 **Warum treiben Sie so gerne diese Sportart?**
Ich bin gern in der frischen Luft / Ich bin gerne Mitglied einer Mannschaft / Ich spiele gern gegen andere, um zu gewinnen / Ich laufe gern / Ich bin gerne unter Freunden / Ich muß mich in Form halten / Es ist wie eine Religion bei uns / Ich habe viel Energie / Es ist ein wenig aggressiv – das habe ich gern!
8 **Beschreiben Sie mir wie man Fußball oder Hockey spielt!**
Es gibt zwei Mannschaften und zwar elf Spieler oder Spielerinnen in; jeder Mannschaft / Man spielt gegen elf Gegner beziehungsweise Gegnerinnen / Man spielt draußen / drinnen / Man benutzt einen Fußball-(Hockey)platz / Es gibt einen Schiedsrichter / zwei Schiedsrichterinnen / Man versucht ein Tor gegen die Opposition zu schießen.

(b) Musikinstrumente
1 **Spielen Sie ein Instrument?**
Nein, ich spiele kein Instrument / Ein wenig. Ich lerne eben / Ja, ich spiele Klavier / Posaune / Geige / Cello / Fagott / Klarinette / Flöte / Bockflöte / Akkordeon / Orgel / Ich bin Schlagzeuger(in).

84 *General conversation*

2 **Wie lange spielen Sie jede Woche?**
Ich übe ... Stunden in der Woche.

3 **Spielen Sie in ein Band oder in einem Orchester?**
Ja, ich bin Mitglied einer Band/eines Orchesters, mit dem Namen ...
Wir spielen Pop, moderne, klassische Musik / Noch nicht / Nein, ich habe keine Zeit dafür.

4 **Wieviele Leute sind in Ihrer Gruppe / Ihrem Band / Ihrem Orchester? Wo und für wen spielen Sie?**
Wir sind ... Spieler und Spielerinnen. Wir spielen im Schulgebäude / in einem Theater / in den Gasthäusern / in einem Sportzentrum / in einer Turnhalle / in den Hotels.

5 **Inwiefern ist Ihre Gruppe / Ihre Band / Ihr Orchester professionnel?**
Bis zu einem gewissen Grade. Um uns zuzuhören, muß man zahlen, aber unser Club, unsere Schule behält das Eintrittsgeld, um neue Instrumente und so weiter zu kaufen und auch zu Wohltätigkeitszwecken.

(*c*) *Wenn Sie abends ausgehen:*

1 **Gehen Sie oft kegeln, oder ins Kino / ins Theater / in das Jugendzentrum / die Diskos?**
Ja ... mal in der Woche / jedes Wochenende / Es kommt darauf an. Wenn ich Geld habe, dann sicher. Sonst, nur dann und wann.

2 **Beschreiben Sie mir einen Besuch dabei!**
Es ist ... Kilometer von hier. In der Stoßzeit muß man Schlange stehen, aber wir können oft im voraus buchen. Es gibt ... große Säle. Es ist ganz modern drinnen / etwas altmodisch. Ich gehe mit Freunden / alleine dahin. Ich bleibe ... Stunden beim Spielen/Schauen dort. Ich esse eine Kleinigkeit, einen Hamburger oder so was. Ich trinke etwas. Dann gehe ich nach Hause, normalerweise gegen ... Uhr.

(*d*) *Radio und Fernsehen*

1 **Könnten wir jetzt über Radio und Fernsehen sprechen. Was haben Sie lieber, Radio oder Fernsehen?**
Keines / Es ist gleich / Ich habe beides gern / Ich ziehe das Radio vor, weil ich irgendwo zuhören kann und es viele verschiedenen Sendungen gibt/Ich sehe lieber fern und das wegen der Farben / weil ich die Dinge gern ansehe / wegen der Sendungen.

2 **Was sind Ihre Lieblingssendungen?**
Ich höre/sehe am liebsten die Sendereihen wie ... / Ich habe die Nachrichtssendungen wie ... gern / Ich liebe Dokumentarfilme / Krimis / Komödien / Liebesgeschichten / Horrorfilme.

3 **Wie lange hören Sie jeden Tag zu/sehen Sie jeden Tag fern?**
Das kann ich nicht sagen / Sagen wir durchschnittlich ... Stunden pro Tag / Es hängt vom Tag und von der Jahreszeit ab / Wenn ich viele Hausaufgaben habe, höre ich nicht zu / sehe ich nicht fern.

4 **Welche Sendungen mögen Sie nicht?**
Ich verabscheue gewaltsame/rassistische/übererotische Themen.

General conversation 85

5 Ihre Bildung
1 **Wie kommen Sie zur Schule?**
 Ich komme zu Fuß / mit dem Bus / mit dem Wagen / mit dem Zug / mit der S-bahn / mit der U-bahn / mit dem Schiff / mit dem Fahrrad / zu Pferd.
2 **Wieviel Zeit brauchen Sie, um in die Schule zu kommen?**
 Etwa ... Minuten / eine Viertelstunde / eine Stunde.
3 **Wo wohnen Sie im Verhältnis zur Schule?**
 (Ich wohne) ... (Kilo)Meter nördlich/südlich/westlich/östlich.
4 **Um wieviel Uhr machen Sie sich auf den Weg zur Schule?**
 Ich verlasse das Haus um ... Uhr ...
5 **Und wielange dauert es?**
 Es dauert sagen wir ... Minuten.
6 **Wann fängt die Schule an?**
 (Sie fängt) um ... Uhr ... (an).
7 **Und wann klingelt es?**
 Um ... Uhr ... / Zu dieser Zeit.
8 **Wie heißt Ihr(e) Klassenlehrer(in)?**
 Er/Sie heißt ...
9 **Und wieviel Pause haben Sie am Tag?**
 (25) Minuten. (20) Minuten morgens und (5) Minuten nachmittags.
10 **Wie oft haben Sie eine Assembly?**
 ... mal in der Woche- Montag, Mittwoch und Freitag / Jeden Tag.
11 **Was für eine Schule besuchen Sie?**
 Sie ist eine Gesamtschule / ein Gymnasium / eine technische Hochschule.
12 **Wieviele Schüler und Schülerinnen gibt es insgesamt?**
 Insgesamt, sagen wir ... hundert, so ungefähr.
13 **Ihre Schule ist für junge Leute in welchem Alter?**
 Sie nimmt Jugendliche zwischen zwölf und achtzehn an.
14 **Wieviele Klassen gibt es?**
 Es sind [6] Klassen pro Jahrgang.
15 **Ist Ihre Schule modern oder alt?**
 Weder modern noch alt / Sehr alt. Sie geht auf achtzehnhundertzwanzig zurück! / Ziemlich modern. Sie wurde neunzehnhundertsechzig gebaut.
16 **Wieviele Schüler und Schülerinnen gibt es in Ihrer Klasse?**
 In meiner Klasse sind wir achtundzwanzig. In meiner Deutschklasse sind wir dreiundzwanzig.
17 **Und in den anderen Klassen?**
 Durchschnittlich, sieben- oder achtundzwanzig in jeder Klasse.
18 **Wieviele Stunden gibt es im Schultag?**
 Wir haben vier Doppelstunden – zwei morgens, zwei nachmittags. Eine Doppelstunde dauert siebzig Minuten.
19 **Um wieviel Uhr hast du Mittagspause?**
 Um zwölf Uhr. Sie dauert knapp ein Stunde.

General conversation

20 Und die anderen Pausen?
Morges und nachmittags haben wir eine Viertelstunde Pause. Morgens um halb elf, nachmittags um zwei Uhr fünfundzwanzig.

21 Welche sind Ihre Lieblingsfächer?
Ich lerne am liebsten ...
Biologie/Chemie/Deutsch/Englisch/Englische Literatur/Erdkunde/Französisch/Geschichte/Handarbeit/Hauswirtschaft/Kochen/Kunst/Latein/Mathe/Musik/Fotographie/Physik/Religion/Spanisch/Sport/Stenographie / Technisches Werken / Maschineschreiben / Turnen / Wirtschaftslehre/Zeichnen.

22 Und welche studieren Sie nicht so gern?
Ich kann ... gar nicht leiden. / Ich habe kein Talent für ...

23 Wer ist Ihr(e) Lieblingslehrer(in)?
Ich habe gar keine / Mir sind all gleich / Sie sind alle sehr sympatisch / Ich kann sie alle nicht leiden / ... kann ich leiden.

24 Warum? / Aus welchem Grund?
Weil er/sie sehr geduldig ist / Da er/sie freundlich / modern ist / Weil er/sie immer schreit! / Weil er/sie mich nachsitzen läßt!

25 Haben Sie jeden Tag viele Hausaufgaben?
Es ist sehr unterschiedlich. Durchschnittlich, drei Fächer, das heißt zweieinhalb Stunden pro Tag / Daß ich nicht lache! Wir haben immer Hausaufgaben, und zuviel!

26 Beschreiben Sie Ihre Schuluniform!
Wir haben gar keine / Sie ist abscheulich! / Sie ist nicht so schlecht / Ich habe sie gern / Die Jungen tragen eine Jacke und einen Pullover ... Die sind blau und haben ein Abzeichen ... Sie tragen auch eine graue Hose und eine gestreifte Krawatte in Blau und Gold ... Die Mädchen tragen eine Bluse, einen Pullover und eine Jacke in den selben Farben. Sie tragen auch einen grauen Rock und weiße Socken ... / In der Oberstufe kann man ... tragen.

27 Sind Sie für oder gegen die Schuluniform?
Ich bin da für/gegen weil ... sie schick/elegant/ ordentlich ist / ich die Farben gern habe / sie anders ist / sie militärisch aussieht / sie zuviel kostet / die Lehrer davon besessen sind / sie altmodisch ist.

28 Beschreiben Sie ein bißchen Ihr Klassenzimmer!
Es gibt ja Platz für ... Personen. Es ist grün gestrichen. Es gibt allerlei Posters und Collagen an den Wänden. Es gibt viele / wenige Fenster. Es hat einen Ausblick auf die Stadt / das Land.

29 Sprechen wir ein bißchen über die Schulvereine und andere Veranstaltungen!
Wir und die Lehrer organisieren eine ganze Menge Clubs und so weiter. Es gibt allerlei Sportvereine, und Vereine für Briefmarken, Schach, Gitarre. Basteln, und Kochen. Wir haben auch einen Chor. Es gibt noch dazu einen Theaterverein, und einen Französisch Kreis, dem ich angehöre. Für die Clubs und fürs Nachsitzen haben wir einen späteren Bus am Mittwochabend.

6 Das Wetter
1 Wie ist das Wetter heute?
Sehr verschieden. Um . . . Uhr hat es geregnet / haben wir Sonne gehabt / hat es geschneit / hat es gefroren / ist es kalt gewesen / haben wir Nebel gehabt / haben wir Tauwetter gehabt / ist es windig gewesen / war das Wetter schön / war das Wetter schlecht / hat es gestürmt / haben wir einen Regenbogen gehabt.

2 Was machen Sie bei schönem Wetter?
Ich gehe gern spazieren / Ich fahre gern mit dem Fahrrad (Auto, Bus, Zug) spazieren / Ich fahre gern Boot auf dem See in der Nähe / Ich gehe fischen, ganz in der Nähe / Ich mache Berg- und Felssteigen mit der Schule / Ich arbeite im Garten / Ich treibe Sport.

3 Und was machen Sie bei schlechtem Wetter?
Ich bleibe zu Hause / Ich mache meine Hausaufgaben / Ich mache die Hausarbeit / Ich gehe im Regen spazieren / Ich verstecke mich irgendwo!

4 Welche Jahreszeit haben Sie am liebsten? Aus welchem Grund?
Ich ziehe den Frühling/Sommer/Herbst/Winter vor. Weil ich die wachsenden Blumen liebe / Weil ich die Sonne und die Hitze so gern habe / Weil ich die wechselnden Farben liebe / Weil ich Schnee und die Nacht sehr mag.

5 Wie ist das Wetter in Deutschland?
Mehr oder weniger wie in Großbritannien, das heißt viel Regen und Nebel im Herbst. Vielleicht bekommen die Deutschen mehr Schnee im Winter, aber es hängt von der Gegend ab, wie bei uns. Nur im Süden, besonders in Bayern kriegen sie viel Sonne im Sommer.

General conversation

7 Die Ferien

1 **Wo verbringen Sie normalerweise Ihre Ferienzeit?**
 Ich bleibe zu Hause / Ich fahre ans Meer / aufs Land / ins Gebirge / ins Seegebiet / in die Großstadt / ins Ausland.

2 **Wohin fahren Sie lieber? Warum?**
 Ich fahre lieber nach … Weil ich die Sonne / die Landschaft / die Einsamkeit / die frische Luft / das Wasser / den Lärm / andere Länder gern habe.

3 **Wohin haben Sie die Absicht dieses Jahr zu fahren?**
 Ich werde höchstwahrscheinlich in … fahren.

4 **Werden Sie alleine fahren?**
 Ja, ich werde alleine sein. / Nein, es wird ein Familienurlaub sein / Nein, ich nehme an einem Schulaustausch teil / Nein, es ist ein Schulbesuch.

5 **Und wie hoffen Sie dorthin zu fahren?**
 Mit dem Wagen (und dem Schiff) / Mit dem Flugzeug / Mit dem Fahrrad / Mit dem Motorrad / Per Anhalter (*oder* ich trampe) / zu Fuß / Mit dem Zug / Mit dem Luxusbus / mit dem Hovercraft.

6 **Werden Sie in einem Hotel schlafen oder was?**
 Nein, bei Freunden / auf dem Campingplatz / in einer Wohnung / in einer Jugendherberge / in einem Landhaus / in einer Pension / in einem Feriendorf / im Zelt / in einem Wohnwagen.

7 **Bei wem werden Sie sich aufhalten?**
 Bei Verwandten/Freunden / einem Bekannten.

8 **Kennen Sie schon ein par deutschsprachige Leute?**
 Ja, meinen Brieffreund / meine Brieffreundin. Er/sie heißt … Ich kenne auch seine/ihre Familie / Ich kenne auch einen, der (eine, die) … heißt.

9 **Wo wohnt er/sie? / Wo wohnen sie?**
 In Nord (Ost, Süd, West) Deutschland (Österreich/Schweiz). Im (Schwarzwald) An der Elbe / am Rhein.

8 Im Ausland

1 Waren Sie schon im Ausland?
Nein, noch nicht / Ja, ich bin nach Deutschland/Spanien/Frankreich gefahren. Ich war ein (zwei, drei) mal da. Ich war neunzehnhundertsiebenundachtzig da.

2 Waren Sie denn alleine?
Ja, ganz alleine / Nein, es war mit der Familie. / Nein, ich war mit einer Schulgruppe. / Nein, ich war Mitglied einer Stadtgruppe in (Frankfurt), unserer Partnerstadt / Ich bin mit einem Freund / einer Freundin hingefahren.

3 In welchem Teil von Deutschlands waren Sie?
Ich habe ... besucht / Ich war in ... / Ich habe meine Zeit in ... verbracht.

4 Wie lange hat Ihren (letzter) Besuch gedauert?
Ich habe drei Tage / eine Woche / vierzehn Tage / zwei Wochen / einen Monat dort verbracht / Ich war zehn Tage da.

5 Wie weit waren Sie von der Großstadt?
Ich war in der Großstadt selbst / Ich war ... Kilometer weit von ...

6 Was haben Sie während Ihres Besuches gemacht?
Ich habe allerlei Dinge gemacht. Ich habe die Sonne / den Schnee / das Wasser ausgenutzt. Unter anderem habe ich historische Gebäude besucht! Auch habe ich viele Leute kennengelernt. Ich habe mich entspannt. Ich habe meine Schularbeit vergessen!

7 Hat Ihnen der Besuch gefallen?
Eben. Ich habe viel Spaß gehabt/Ich habe mich gut amüsiert/Er war ein großer Erfolg / Teils ja, teils nein / Er hat seine Vorteile und seine Nachteile gehabt / Er war unheimlich toll! / Ohne weiteres! Ich fahre nächstes Jahr zurück / Tatsächlich, nein.

8 Warum?
Es war wirklich eine Abwechslung / Das Essen hat mir sehr gut (schlecht) gefallen! / Ich habe die Deutschen (Österreicher, Schweizer, Franzosen, Spanier), die ich getroffen habe, sehr gern / Das Leben / Die Lebensart gefällt mir / Ich habe gute Freunde kennengelernt / Die Familie war sehr gastfreundlich.

9 Welche Unterschiede zwischen dort und hier haben Sie bemerkt?
Die Schule fängt früher an und endet früher / Die Geschäfte machen früher auf und schleißen später. Man ißt und trinkt mehr. Vielleicht ißt man mehr Fett. Es gibt mehr Wohnungen und Wohnblocks und weniger Ein- und Zweifamilienhäuser. Im Süden ist es wärmer. Die Straßen sind nicht so schmutzig wie bei uns. Die Leute sind pünktlicher.

90 *General conversation*

9 Eine Zeitfrage

1 Was haben Sie gestern abend gemacht?
Zuerst habe ich meine Hausaufgaben gemacht / Ich habe gestrickt / Ich mußte eine Stunde in der Schule nachsitzen! / Ich habe Freunde angerufen / Ich habe Platten und Kassetten gehört / Ich habe die normale Hausarbeit gemacht / Ich bin (mit Freunden) ausgegangen / Ich bin in die (Groß)Stadt gegangen / Ich habe ferngesehen / Ich bin zum Verein (Klub) gegangen.

2 Was haben Sie letzten Samstag gemacht?
Ich bin etwas später als normalerweise aufgestanden / Ich habe ausgeschlafen / Ich bin zu / nach . . . mit Freunden gegangen / Ich habe Einkäufe gemacht / Ich habe Sport getrieben / Ich habe gebastelt.

END OF BASIC WORK

---

3 Was werden Sie nächsten Sonntag machen?
Ich werde zur Kirche gehen / Ich werde lange im Bett bleiben / Ich werde Briefe schreiben / Ich werde das Mittagessen vorbereiten / Ich werde . . . spielen / Ich werde Freunde besuchen / Ich werde überhaupt nichts machen! / Das wird vom Wetter und meiner Familie abhängen / Ich werde spazieren gehen (fahren).

4 Was werden Sie nach den Prüfungen machen?
So wenig wie möglich! / Ich werde Urlaub machen / Ich werde eine Stelle (einen Job) finden / Ich werde Bücher lesen, die ich gern habe / Ich werde viel Sport treiben / Ich werde zu Rock-Konzerten im Freien gehen / Ich werde an einem Austausch teilnehmen.

5 Was werden Sie machen, wenn Sie die Schule verlassen?
Ich werde zwei Jahre in der Oberstufe verbringen / Ich werde eine Lehre als . . . machen / Ich werde einen YOPS-Kurs machen / Ich glaube, ich werde auswandern / Ich werde einen Beruf finden / Vielleicht werde ich arbeitslos werden / Ich werde mich zurechtfinden / Ich werde ein kleines Geschäft aufmachen / Ich werde nichts zu tun haben.

6 Was würden Sie machen, wenn Sie reich wären?
Ich würde mein Geld benutzen, um den armen Leuten der Welt zu helfen / Ich würde nicht arbeiten / Ich würde eine Weltreise mit dem Schiff machen / Ich würde eine ganze Menge Kleider kaufen / Ich würde gegen das Böse der Welt kämpfen / Ich würde in Deutschland wohnen! / Ich würde wohnen, wo ich wollte.

7 Was würden Sie machen, wenn Sie nicht zur Schule gehen sollten?
Ich würde *das* machen, was *mir* gefällt! / Ich würde mich in der Sonne bräunen / Ich würde Billard spielen / Ich würde meine Schuluniform verbrennen!

8 Was würden Sie für ein Unfallsopfer auf der Straße machen?
Erstens würde ich auf keinen Fall den Menschen berühren! / Ich würde den Arzt beziehungsweise die Ärztin rufen / Ich würde einen Sanitätswagen rufen.

SPEAKING
Situation narrative 1

Describing your holiday
Imagine this map shows your holiday in West Germany last year. Talk about the journey and what happened on it.

Specimen answer
Beschreiben Sie mir bitte Ihre Ferien in Deutschland

Wir sind Samstag um elf Uhr abgefahren, mit dem Wagen. Was kann ich euch sagen? . . . Na, ja, es war ein schöner Morgen, viel Sonnenschein und wir waren gegen fünfzehn Uhr in Dover. Dann sind wir mit der Fähre von Dover nach Zeebrugge gefahren. Die Überfahrt hat ja so ungefähr zwei Stunden gedauert. Dann sind wir mit dem Wagen weitergefahren und wir sind ziemlich spät in Aachen angekommen . . . sagen wir gegen zehn Uhr abends. Es war auch zu spät, wir waren alle totmüde. Es war aber ein schönes Hotel und da haben wir übernachtet.

Am Sonntag sind wir bis Frankfurt weitergefahren und das war nicht besonders spät. Dieses Mal war es sieben Uhr oder so ähnlich und wir fanden eine Pension. Die Leute da waren so unheimlich nett, daß wir dort drei Tage geblieben sind.

Am Mittwoch um acht Uhr abends waren wir in Stuttgart. Das Gasthaus war auch prima! Wir haben noch einmal sehr gut gegessen und getrunken.

Am Donnerstag um fünf Uhr waren wir endlich am Ziel. Endlich! Da haben wir sieben Tage gezeltet. Wir hatten Glück-es gab vielzutun. Ich bin viel geritten und im Freibad gewesen. Die anderen machten andere Dinge. Ich aber habe historische Gebäude nicht gern! Ich war lieber im Wasser!

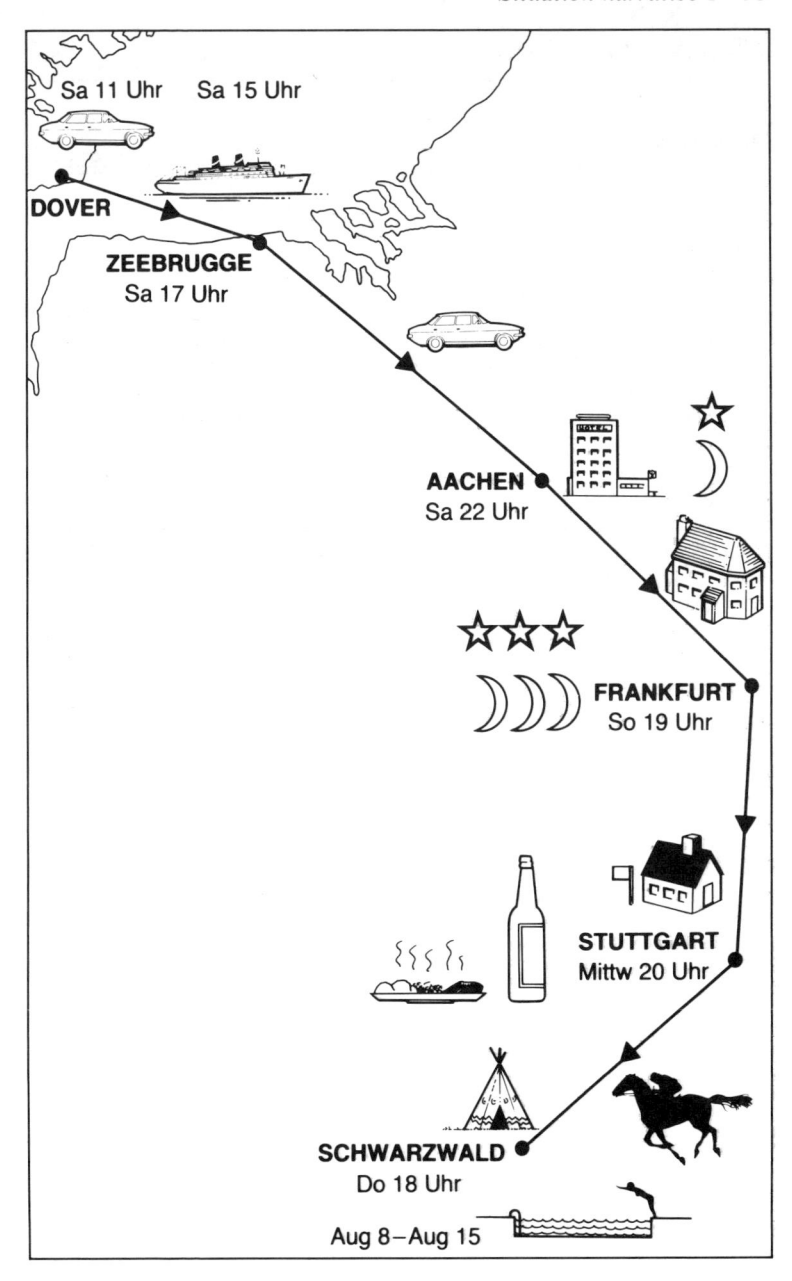

Situation narrative 1 93

Sa 11 Uhr   Sa 15 Uhr

DOVER

ZEEBRUGGE
Sa 17 Uhr

AACHEN
Sa 22 Uhr

FRANKFURT
So 19 Uhr

STUTTGART
Mittw 20 Uhr

SCHWARZWALD
Do 18 Uhr

Aug 8 – Aug 15

SPEAKING
Situation narrative 2

Describing a break-down
You were on holiday in the Federal Republic a few weeks ago. Describe your trip and the break-down:

Specimen answer
Erzählen Sie mir bitte, was Ihnen in Deutschland passiert ist!

Wir haben am zwanzigsten Juli um acht Uhr Stratford verlassen . . . das war der Anfang unserer Ferienreise. Wir haben einige Stauprobleme gehabt, aber wir haben immerhin unseren Flug um zehn Uhr dreißig zum Birmingham Flughafen geschafft. Dann sind wir um Viertel vor eins in Düsseldorf gelandet. Keine Angst – der Flug hat keineswegs zweieinviertel Stunden gedauert! Im Sommer gehen die Uhren in Deutschland eine Stunde vor!

Wir haben da zu Mittag gegessen und getrunken und sind mit einem Hertz-Wagen bis Kleindorf weitergefahren. Dort haben wir fast zwei Wochen bei Freunden verbracht. Sie haben einen schönen alten Bauernhof und mein Bruder und ich haben viel Spaß gehabt. Und wissen Sie was? Ich bin zum ersten Mal auf einem Pferd geritten! Das war aber prima! Mein Bruder hat auf dem See gerudert, das ist aber nichts für mich.

Dann haben wir am zweiten August diese verdammte Panne gehabt! Es ist eine alte Geschichte – ein Steinchen auf der Landstraße, eine zersplitterte Windschutzscheibe, ein Abschleppwagen und dreihundert Deutschmark später eine neue Scheibe. Das problem war, als wir in Koblenz angekommen sind, hatten wir kein deutsches Geld mehr! Die Eltern waren sehr schlechter Laune!

Situation narrative 2 95

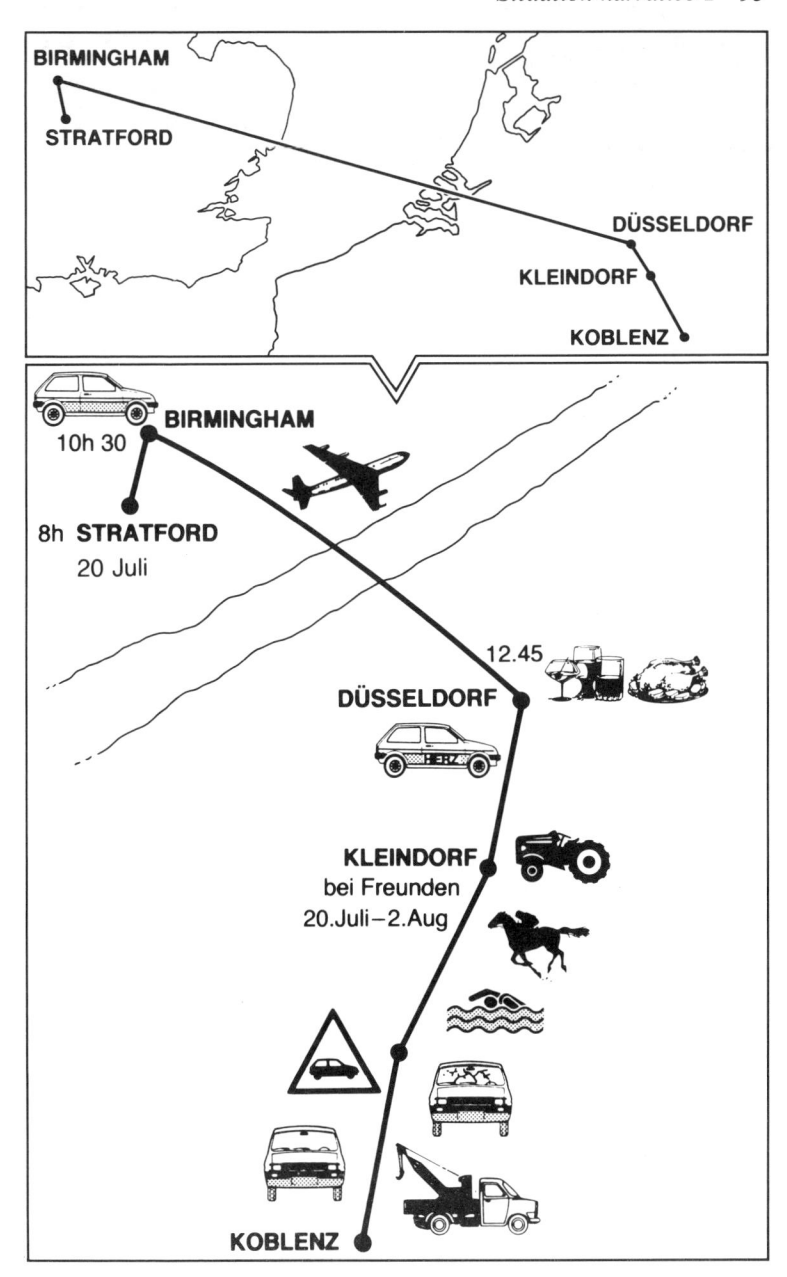

WRITING

General hints

As with the other three skills, the Writing Papers are out to discover what you can do, *not* to set traps to find out what you don't know! You will therefore be given credit for straightforward, *reasonably* accurate written German, which gets your message across.

Remember that the kinds of written tasks you have to fulfil have been designed to be useful to you in the real world outside your class and exam room.

For this very good reason, what you write will be judged not on whether whole strings of words are correct. Instead, the question will be: *Has this person communicated his/her message effectively?* If the answer in your case is *Yes*, then you should obtain high marks for the task.

With this in mind, read through the following hints and try to apply them when you write:

1. Before you do anything else, look at the task in front of you and ask yourself *exactly* what you are required to do.
2. If the task asks for specific information, make sure you give it. For example, if a letter to which you have to reply contains five questions, be certain to answer each one.
3. Work within the framework of the task. If, for instance, you have to write a small ad., don't let it develop into a mini-essay.
4. Pay attention to the time limits. Of all the four Tests, Writing is the one where you will normally be under the greatest pressure of time. The time given is not generous, so time yourself.
5. Make a *brief rough plan* of what you are going to write.
6. Produce a final version based on the rough plan.
7. Leave yourself a few minutes at the end, to check right through everything you have written for errors.

For the Basic Level, you will be marked on your ability to get your message across, so do not be afraid that you will be heavily penalised if you are not totally accurate in your spelling, etc. You will often be required to provide one-, two- and three-word answers to lists, diary items and so on. In replies to postcards, small ads, etc., you will on no occasion be required to write more than 60 words.

For the Higher Level, you will be required to write answers of approximately 100 or 130 words (depending on the Board for whose exam you are preparing).

We have frequently included a *specimen answer* to help you. Whenever possible, try to produce your own answer to the small ad, postcard, letter, etc., *before* looking at the model.

WRITING
1 Postcards 1

Answering a postcard is an activity which most people can do well, if they remember to include all the items they are asked and look carefully at the card. The way it is shaped and written will often help you with your answer.

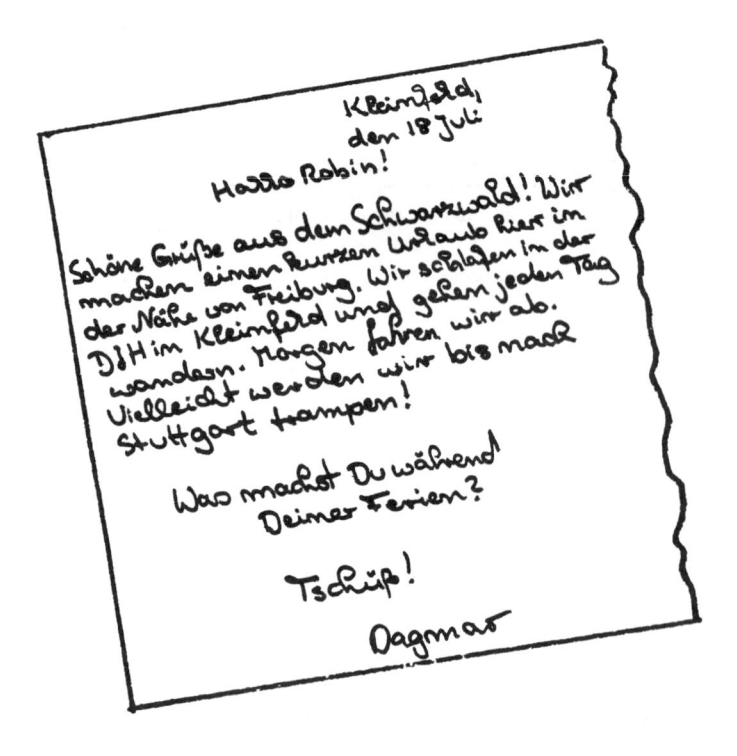

> Kleinfeld,
> den 18 Juli
>
> Hallo Robin!
>
> Schöne Grüße aus dem Schwarzwald! Wir machen einen kurzen Urlaub hier in der Nähe von Freiburg. Wir schlafen in der DJH in Kleinfeld und gehen jeden Tag wandern. Morgen fahren wir ab. Vielleicht werden wir bis nach Stuttgart trampen!
>
> Was machst Du während Deiner Ferien?
>
> Tschüß!
> Dagmar

Aufgabe A few days after receiving this postcard, you go on holiday to the Lake District. Send a card to Dagmar in reply, thanking her for her card, saying that you are at a boarding house, telling her that you are going boating on a lake tomorrow, and that you are travelling around by bike.

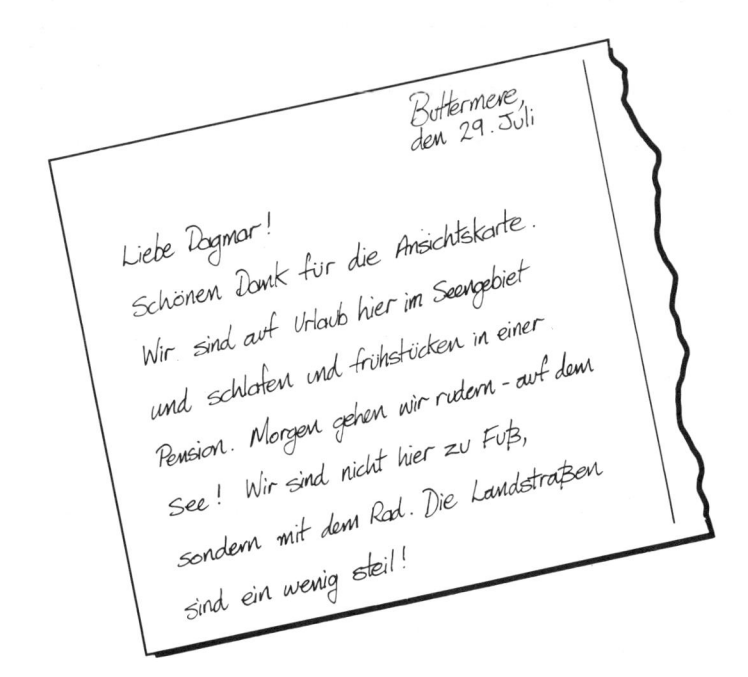

Postcards 99

> Buttermere, den 29. Juli
>
> Liebe Dagmar!
> Schönen Dank für die Ansichtskarte. Wir sind auf Urlaub hier im Seengebiet und schlafen und frühstücken in einer Pension. Morgen gehen wir rudern – auf dem See! Wir sind nicht hier zu Fuß, sondern mit dem Rad. Die Landstraßen sind ein wenig steil!

tips!
1 Don't be afraid to take the shape of some of your phrases from the card you are answering.
2 This candidate has been confident enough to introduce a short extra comment which is very suitable and quite humorous.
3 Most important of all, see how he has made sure he has mentioned all the things he was asked.

WRITING
2 Diary

Filling in your diary is a Basic exercise you may have to do. There will usually be one example item, with perhaps some other information. Use other information. Use the example (here it's *Sa 29*) as a guide to how you should write your entries.

Aufgabe Your German-speaking pen-friend is coming to stay with you for a fortnight, starting on the last-but-one day of the Summer Term.

Juli	
So 23	So 30 ....
Mo 24 *Friedrich kommt an*	Mo 31 ....
Di 25 *Letzter Schultag*	**August** Di 1 ....
Mi 26	Mi 2 ....
Do 27	Do 3 ....
Fr 28	Fr 4 ....
Sa 29 *Zum Fußballspiel*	Sa 5 ....

Fill in this double page from your diary with eight interesting things you might do:

Juli

So 23 ....

Mo 24 ....*Friedrich kommt an*....

Di 25 ....*Letzter Schultag*....
Friedrich kommt mit!

Mi 26 ....

Do 27 ....*Kegeln*....

Fr 28 ....*In die Disko*....

Sa 29 ....*Zum Fußballspiel*....

So 30 ....*Zur Kirche*....

Mo 31 ....*Zum Hallenbad*....

August Di 1 ....

Mi 2 ....*Ans Meer*....

Do 3 ....*Zum Bahnmuseum*....

Fr 4 ....

Sa 5 ....*Ins Kino*....

Specimen answer

tips!

Notice how this candidate has chosen straightforward activities, which she is confident she can write down.

See how she has put down the right-place words in Juli 28, 30, 31, Aug. 2, 3, 5. Juli 25: A good idea to take Friedrich to school.

WRITING
3 Postcards 2

Nothing particularly interesting has happened to the writer of this card. Write a reply saying there's a lot going on in your town, you're playing hockey for the school, you will phone Stephan before long, and asking if he would please send you some stamps for your collection.

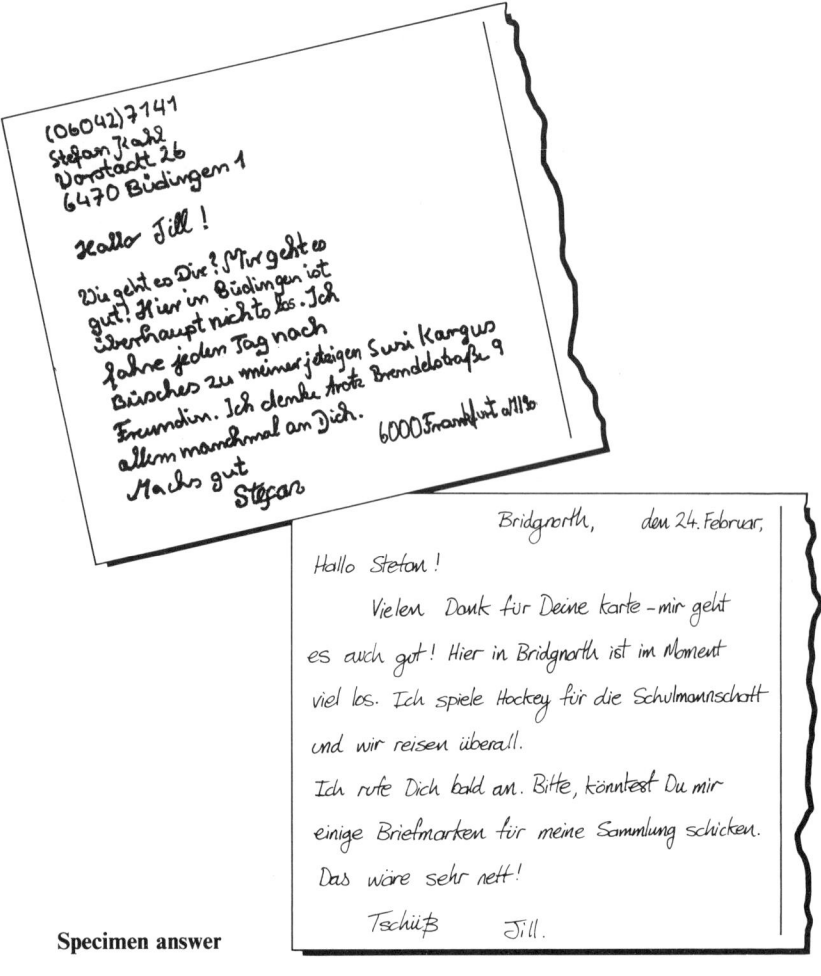

(06042) 7141
Stefan Kahl
Vorstadt 26
6470 Büdingen 1

Hallo Jill!

Wie geht es Dir? Mir geht es gut! Hier in Büdingen ist überhaupt nichts los. Ich fahre jeden Tag nach Büsches zu meiner jetzigen Freundin. Ich denke trotz allem manchmal an Dich.
Mach's gut
Stefan

Susi Kargus
Brendelstraße 9
6000 Frankfurt a/Mo.

Bridgnorth, den 24. Februar,

Hallo Stefan!

Vielen Dank für Deine Karte – mir geht es auch gut! Hier in Bridgnorth ist im Moment viel los. Ich spiele Hockey für die Schulmannschaft und wir reisen überall.
Ich rufe Dich bald an. Bitte, könntest Du mir einige Briefmarken für meine Sammlung schicken. Das wäre sehr nett!
Tschüß Jill.

Specimen answer

A very well-written card. Jill does everything she is asked here. She also shows politeness, and includes a little extra relevant information.

WRITING
4 Postcards 3

Write a postcard replying to Marika Burkard. Say you cannot phone from home, because your phone is not working. You have tried five times from a friend's house, but you got no answer. Suggest you meet at the station.

> Ich habe Ihre Anzeige gestern im Kreisanzeiger gelesen und Sie sofort angerufen. Da aber bei Ihnen keiner da war, möchte ich Sie bitten, wenn Sie mich anrufen würden, sobald Sie daheim sind.
>
> Mit freundlichen Grüßen
> Marika Burkard
>
> Ich bin unter folgender Telefonnummer zu erreichen: 0604297873

Specimen answer

> den 14. September
>
> Es tut mir leid aber ich kann Sie nicht von zu Hause anrufen, da das Telefon nicht funktioniert. Ich war bei meinem Freund und ich habe da fünfmal versucht mit Ihnen zu sprechen. Leider habe ich keine Antwort bekommen. Könnten wir uns vielleicht am Treffpunkt am Bahnhof treffen?
> Mit freundlichen Grüßen!
> Delme Hopkins

A very competent and impressive reply. Delme scored credit in every way with this card.

Firstly, he picked up the fact that Marika Burkard (a) gave no indication as to whether she was a *Frau* or *Fräulein*, (b) did not start with a greeting, and dealt with the situation appropriately.

Note also his confident use of quite straightforward language.

Additionally, he doesn't make the same mistake as Marika with her capitals. (Don't worry, this sort of error won't creep in in the actual exam!). His good vocabulary helps him make short work of suggesting the meeting (4).

WRITING
5 A holiday invitation

Write a short letter (70 words) in German to Karin/Uwe, thanking him/her for the letter and accepting an invitation to go on a bike-trip round Holland. Ask . . .
> What the intended dates are
> Should you bring your own bike
> Or should you hire one
> The approximate cost
> For a quick reply to your letter.

Pen-y-Bont ar Ogwr,
den 22. Juni

Liebe Karin!

Recht schönen Dank für Deinen letzten Brief. Ja, bitte, das würde mir viel Spaß machen, eine Radtour mit Euch zu machen.

Natürlich habe ich einige Fragen - vielleicht kannst Du mir ziemlich schnell Antworten darauf geben:

1) Welche Daten hast du vor? Für mich wäre es besser im August.
2) Soll ich mein Rad mitbringen, oder ist es möglich, eins da zu mieten?
3) Wieviel wird das kosten, so ungefähr?

Laß bitte bald von Dir hören!
Dein Freund
Robin.

Specimen answer

tips!

1. Robin has dealt with all seven points. So, he has made a very good start towards achieving a good grade.
2. Perhaps extra credit for accepting the invitation *enthusiastically*.
3. Not only does he ask for the intended dates, he also suggests what he prefers. This shows good self-confidence and the ability to communicate his own position. He gets credit for this.
4. He combines the questions about the bikes well into one clear sentence.
5. When asking about the cost, he shows he can talk and write in the future, for which he will again get credit.
6. He shows a good sense of urgency, by emphasising for the second time (but in different words) the need for Karin to write quickly.

Over-all impression: A first-class, direct answer, using straightforward, sensible language.

WRITING
6 Postcards 4

Reply to Ulrich's card, making sure you answer all the points raised.

> Hallo, Paula!
>
> Hast Du am 23.11 was vor? Wenn nicht, dann komm' doch zu mir. Ich veranstalte eine kleine Fête, habe aber nichts zu trinken... Es wird ziemlich lange dauern. Wer Lust hat, kann bei mir schlafen. Morgens gibt's dann ein Katerfrühstück.
> Also, bis dann!
> Ulrich

> Dortmund, den 14. November.
>
> Lieber Ulrich!
>
> Ich danke Dir recht herzlich für die Einladung! Am 23.11 bin ich total frei! Keine Sorge, ich werde einige Dosen Cola mitbringen! Ja, danke, ich möchte gern bei Dir schlafen und ich esse nie Frühstück!
> Bis bald!
> Paula.

Specimen answer

This is a good example of a fairly brief reply which answers all the points most adequately.

Paula starts well by writing down a sensible date, having noted the one mentioned by Ulrich.

She uses a more ambitious form of thank-you which suggests confidence.

Keine Sorge is a most appropriate exclamation and she follows this up with a confident use of the Future Tense.

A touch of humour, answering the question of breakfast adds interest to the card.

WRITING
7 Postcards 5

Reply to Bianca's card, saying you have been to the Lost Property Office, but Bianca's keep-sake had not been handed in. Say you will go back there again on Friday evening next week. You will phone Saturday next week to let Bianca know.

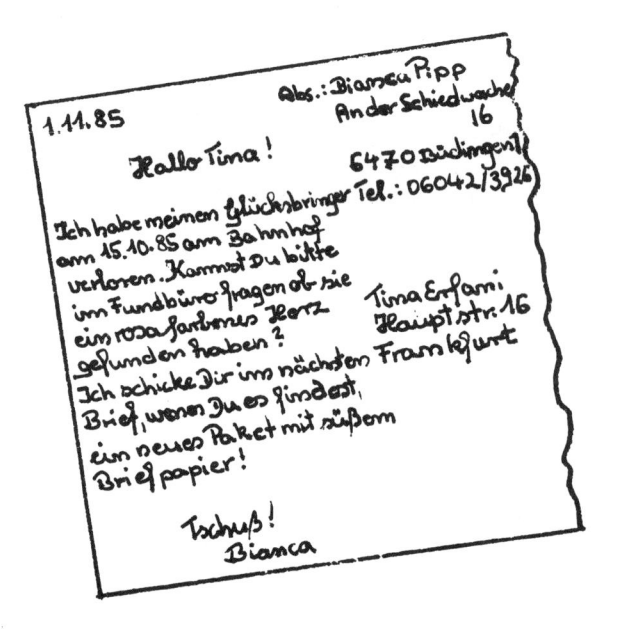

> 1.11.85
>
> Abs.: Bianca Pipp
> An der Schiedwache 16
> 6470 Büdingen
> Tel.: 06042/3926
>
> Hallo Tina!
>
> Ich habe meinen Glücksbringer am 15.10.85 am Bahnhof verloren. Kannst Du bitte im Fundbüro fragen ob sie ein rosafarbenes Herz gefunden haben?
> Ich schicke Dir im nächsten Brief, wenn Du es findest, ein neues Paket mit süßem Briefpapier!
>
> Tina Erfami
> Hauptstr. 16
> Frankfurt
>
> Tschüß!
> Bianca

> 10.11.85
>
> Hallo Bianca!
> Ich habe schlechte Nachrichten für Dich! Niemand ist zum Fundbüro mit deinem Glücksbringer gekommen aber ich werde nächste Woche am Freitag abend wieder dahingehen. Am Somstag abend werde ich Dich anrufen, damit Du weißt.
> Auf Wiederhören!
> Deine Freundin,
> Tina.

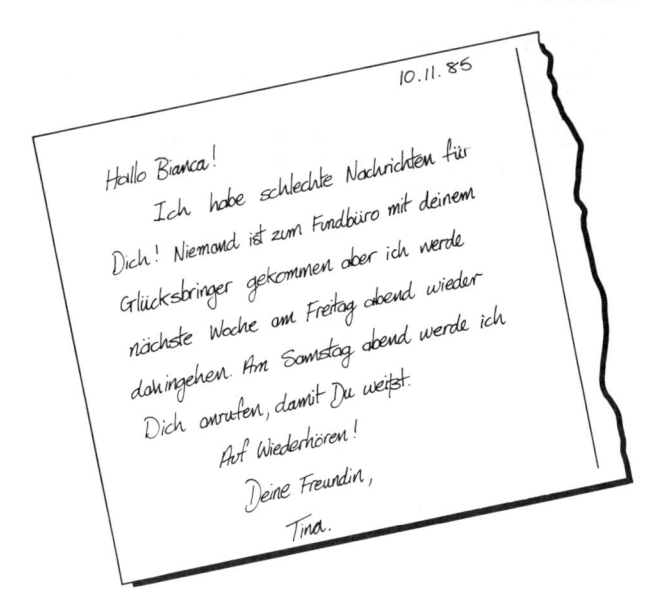

Specimen answer

Again a very competent and self-confident reply. Tina starts off with an appropriate, rather emotional expression.

She deals very well with *handed-in,* by using natural and straightforward German.

She, too, uses the Future Tense well, to communicate exactly the right message. Tina uses *damit* (so that) well, to give the idea of *letting know*.

She shows her good command of German with an appropriate farewell greeting.

However, although it is assumed from the beginning that she has actually been to the Lost Property office, it would have been as well to mention it, as asked.

WRITING
8 Booking accommodation

This is one of the most common types of letter you may have to write. You may also find that you have to compose all of the letter, without having one in front of you to answer.

Once again, the most important thing is to cover **all** the points you are asked to put in. As you write your letter, keep checking against the list of points in the question, to make sure you do everything asked of you. You will probably gain marks for this.

Try the *Aufgabe* below, and compare your letter with the specimen opposite. Afterwards, learn the typical phrases (underlined) which you need when booking rooms, etc.

Aufgabe Write a letter (70 words) to the manager of a holiday hotel in a German-speaking country, thanking him for his brochure and asking for the following:

two double-bedrooms from 11–25 August, inclusive,
one of these with a bathroom and fridge,
the other with a shower,
full board, with breakfast in bed,
brochures about the region, so you can plan your trips.

Booking accommodation 109

> Ealing,
> den 15. Juni
>
> <u>Sehr geehrter Herr Leiter!</u>
>
> <u>Wir haben Ihre Broschüre dankend erhalten</u>, könnten wir jetzt bitte folgendes buchen?
>
> Wir möchten zwei Zweibettzimmer haben und zwar <u>zwischen 11. und 25. August (inklusiv).</u> Wir brauchen bitte ein Zimmer mit Bad und Kühlschrank und eins mit Dusche.
>
> Auch möchten wir <u>Voll-Pension mit Frühstück im Schlafzimmer. Würden Sie auch so nett sein,</u> uns einige Prospekte über die Region zu schicken, damit wir unsere Ausflüge <u>im vorausplanen</u> können?
>
> <u>Hochachtungsvoll!</u>
> Carolyn Burch.

Specimen answer

tips!

1 The writer has included all the points asked.
2 She has also kept closely to the total number of words requested.
3 Several phrases show how polite she is. With politeness, she is more likely to get what she wants.
4 The use of paragraphs to split up the ideas helps her letter to be very clear and easy to understand.

WRITING
9 Postcards 6

Reply to Katrin and Frank thanking them for their invitation, which you accept with pleasure. Say you will get there at 6 pm on the 2nd May and would be grateful to be met at the station. Also ask what they would like for a present.

> Hallo Christine!
>
> Zu unserer Verlobung am 4. Mai 1986 laden wir Dich ganz herzlich ein! Ab 15 Uhr feiern wir im Büdinger Berghof. Wir freuen uns auf Dein Kommen!
>
> Katrin Zindahl
> Frank Weider

> den 15. April, 1988.
>
> Liebe Katrin! Lieber Frank!
> Meinen besten Dank für die Einladung zur Verlobung ich freue mich schon darauf! Ich werde am 2. Mai ankommen und ich würde sehr dankbar sein, wenn ihr mich vom Hauptbahnhof um 18:00 Uhr abholen könntet.
> Die Hauptfrage - Was für ein Geschenk möchtet ihr haben? Ruft mich doch an!
> Einen schönen Kuß!
> Christine.

Specimen answer

Christine starts well by remembering to write a separate greeting for each of Katrin and Frank, because there are two genders.

She makes good use of a lively expression to express her acceptance.

The candidate handles the *ihr* Form (with its characteristic *t* ending) well. Remember to practise writing to two people, as well as to one.

A good use of appropriate vocabulary.

A very competent, lively postcard.

END OF BASIC WORK

WRITING
10 Writing to an information office

This is the sort of letter with which you might be asked to deal, by people in official positions who have no German, but know that you do! Here, you are helping out the local Tourist Office. See how good a job you can do for your town! (approx 100 words).

Sehr geehrter Leiter des Informationsamtes

Wir sind fünfzig Leute in Ihrer Partnerstadt und bitten Sie, uns Auskunft über die Stadt und unsere Unterkunft zu geben. Wir möchten auch noch wissen ob es in Ihrer Stadt auch Möglichkeiten gibt Sport zu treiben oder in die Oper, das Konzert oder das Theater zu gehen. Wir möchten auch erfahren ob es noch Sehenswürdigkeiten außerhalb Ihrer Stadt gibt und man mit einem Bus oder Bahn dorthin kommen kann. Sie können uns auch gleich die Preise mitschicken, wir würden uns sehr freuen wenn Sie uns Informationen schicken würden.

Thorsten Lenz

Specimen answer

> den 19. Juni
>
> Sehr geehrter Herr Lenz!
>
> Wir haben dankend Ihren Brief erhalten und schicken Ihnen hierbei Prospekte und Broschüren über die Stadt und Ihre Unterkunft, Preise usw.
>
> Peterborough hat eine ganze Menge Sport-und Kulturmöglichkeiten und die Universitätsstadt Cambridge ist nicht sehr weit von hier.
>
> Was Sehenswürdigkeiten betrifft, haben wir das Sumpfgebiet in der Nähe und die Nordsee auch. Mit dem Bus oder der Bahn ist das kein Problem. Preise und andere Auskunft sind in den Prospekten.
>
> Hochachtungsvoll!
>
> Peterborough Tourist Office.

This candidate has learnt business-letter expressions very well (paragraph 1). He scores very high marks for answering all the points in the letter. Once or twice he drops into the casual language we all use with our friends (paragraph 2), but still gains much credit, because he has communicated his thoughts accurately. He has also done his swotting on his own local area (paragraph 3). His neat paragraphing makes his letter easy to read. Excellent.

WRITING
11 Telling a story 1

Tell the story of each of the following sets of pictures. You may find it easier to write as if you are one of the characters.

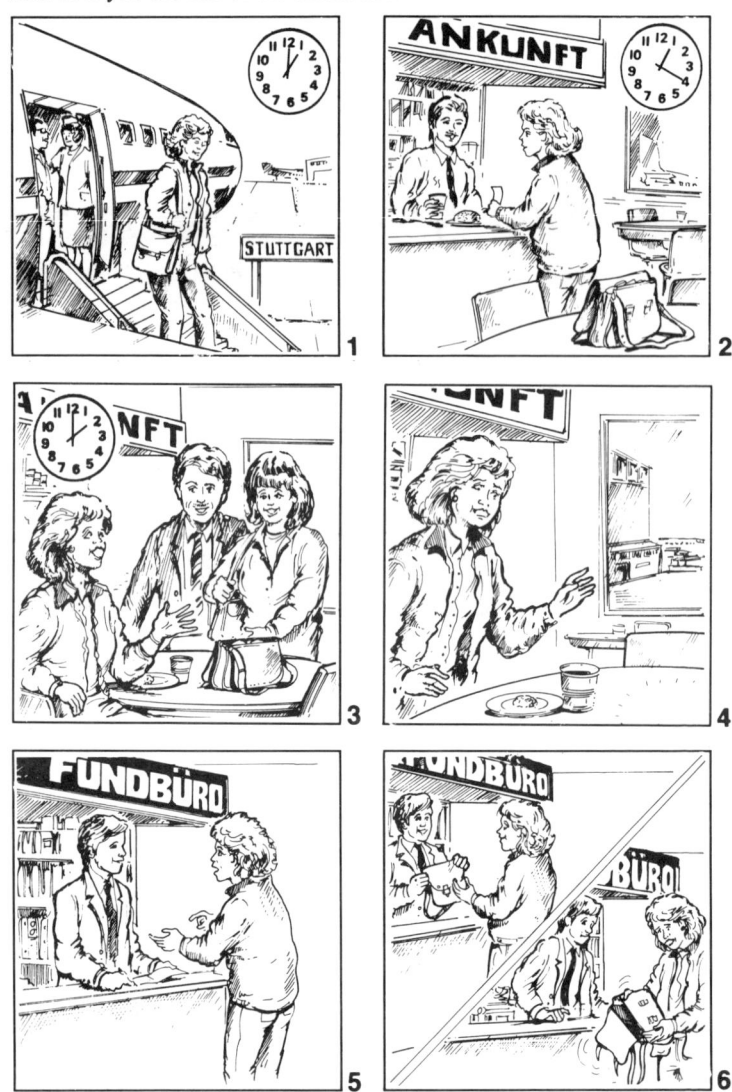

Specimen answer

Eines Sommertages befand ich mich rechtzeitig am Stuttgarter Flughafen, aber ich mußte warten, da meine deutschen Gastgeber noch nicht da waren, um mich abzuholen. Deshalb habe ich mir eine heiße Schokolade und einen Berliner gekauft.

Nach einer Stunde und einer Reifenpanne auf dem Wege sind meine Freunde endlich gekommen und nachdem wir uns begrüßt hatten, habe ich bemerkt, daß meine Handtasche verschwunden war.

Ich wußte nicht, was ich machen sollte. „Gehen wir zum Fundbüro!" schlug Frau Holz vor. „Vielleicht wirst du sie da finden."

Im Fundbüro habe ich meine Tasche dem Beamten beschrieben und er hat sie mir geholt. Einen Augenblick war ich sehr glücklich, aber das hat nicht lange gedauert – meine Tasche war leer!

WRITING
12 Telling a story 2

Specimen answer

"Wir laden Dich zu unserer Hochzeit ein!;; So haben Gabi und Rudi mir geschrieben und deshalb habe ich einige Tage später in München den Frankfurter Zug genommen.

Gegen elf machten einige Rowdys Krawall auf einer Brücke, indem sie große Steine auf die Bahn worfen, aber glücklicherweise hat unser Zugführer die Steine gesehen und unseren TEE gestoppt.

Die Bahnreparatur hat ungefähr vierzig Minuten gedauert und, da ich jetzt verspätet war, mußte ich zur Kirche laufen, weil es kein Taxi am Bahnhof gab!

Kein Wunder, daß ich angekommen bin, während die Braut in die Kirche eintrat. Sie und ihr Vater haben gewartet, bis ich meinen Platz gefunden hatte. Um ein Haar!

WRITING
13 Telling a story 3

Specimen answer

Ich trämpe gern und war dabei, mit der Fähre über Zeebrugge nach Deutschland zu fahren, als ich Ute in der Bar getroffen habe.

Wir plauderten zusammen, als zwei schöne Jungen angefangen haben, mit uns zu sprechen, aber da wir beide einen Freund zu Hause hatten, haben wir sie fortgeschickt.

Nach Zeebrugge haben wir Probleme gehabt, da die Fahrer keine Lust hatten, uns zu helfen. Es gab auch eine Hitzewelle und wir würden vielleicht einen Sonnenbrand gekriegt haben, ohne die zwei Jungen, die angehalten haben, um uns mitzunehmen.

Noch dazu haben sie alles für uns erledigt – wir haben bei ihnen und ihren Eltern übernachtet. Es waren nette Leute!

LANGUAGE POINTS

Language Points is not a traditional grammar revision section. Instead, it is intended to be used together with the ordinary grammar that you will find in your school text-book.

Think of the grammar you have learnt as the building-blocks which allow you to put words together in the right shapes and in a sensible order. These groups of words describe *ideas*. The *Language Points* are those *ideas* put together in groups that once again make sense. Let's look at a concrete example.

Imagine you have to **apologise** for some minor mishap. You will probably start off by a **polite greeting** of some sort. After your apology, it is likely that the other person will **forgive** you and try to ease your feelings. You may then offer to **undo the damage**. Your offer will be **accepted/declined**.

If you look through the sections in the *Language Points*, you will see that there are lists of ways of communicating all these ideas. In fact, the *Language Points* are grouped together in blocks of ideas, like the one we've just worked through, in the likely order of a short conversation.

If you think about what we've just done, you will see that we can often predict the order of ideas in a straightforward conversation. This should help you to think ahead as to what is likely to come up in a conversation when speaking German, rather in the way that a chess-player has to try and think four or five moves ahead in a game of chess.

But we all know life is not quite as simple as that. Other human beings don't always react to what we say in the way we expect. Again, your *Language Points* should be able to help you. If, for example, someone gets very irritated, when you expected a polite reply, you should be in a position to know how to react to irritation in German.

When you work through the *Language Points*, get a friend to practise each string of ideas with you. You will find that they provide you with a basis for many lively conversations. *Viel Glück!*

LANGUAGE POINTS
1 Asking people to repeat, explain, or say something more clearly

Wie bitte? ⎫
Bitte? ⎬ Pardon?
Was war das? — What was that?
Was! — What!
Kannst du das wiederholen? — Can you repeat that?
Können Sie das erklären? — Can you explain that?
Kannst du das buchstabieren? — Can you spell that?
Wie schreibt man das? — How do you spell that?
Wie meinst du das? — How do you mean?
Ich habe das nicht kapiert! — I didn't understand that!
Das habe ich nicht ganz verstanden — I didn't quite understand that
Wie sagt man . . . auf Deutsch? — How do you say . . . In German?
Was bedeutet . . . auf Englisch? — What's . . . in English?

LANGUAGE POINTS
2 Asking questions

***Was** hast du gesagt?* — **What** did you say?
***Wo** kann ich einen Arzt finden?* — **Where** can I find a doctor?
***Woher** weißt du das?* — **Where** do you know that from?
***Welches** Foto hast du lieber?* — **Which** photo do your prefer?
***Wer** ist sie?* — **Who** is she?
***Wann** kommst du wieder?* — **When** are you coming back (again)?

***Wie** komme ich zur Post?* — **How** do I get to the post-office?
***Wie** lange brauche ich?* — **How** long do I need?
***Warum** spielst du nicht mit?* — **Why** aren't you playing?

LANGUAGE POINTS
3 Making sure someone understands

Alles klar? — Are you clear?
Bist du darüber klar? — Are you clear on that?
Ist das klar? — Is that clear?
Kapiert? — Got it?
Einverstanden? — Are we agreed?
Soll ich wierderholen? — Shall I repeat it?
Soll ich erklären? — Shall I explain?
Hast du alles verstanden/kapiert? — Have you understood it all?

LANGUAGE POINTS
4 Asking others whom or what they know

Weißt du, daß.. . . ? — Do you know that . . . ?
Weißt du (hier) Bescheid? — Do you know (all) about it?
Hat man dir Bescheid gesagt? — Have you been told?
Hast du es begriffen? — Have you got it?
Hast du eine Ahnung? — Have you any idea?
Was soll das vorstellen? — What's it supposed to be?
Die kennst du schon? — Have you already met her?
Kennst du den nicht? — Don't you know him?

LANGUAGE POINTS
5 Saying if you know something or someone

Das ist doch klar!	That's pretty obvious!
Das weiß ich (ganz) bestimmt!	I know that for definite
Das weiß ich (doch) genau	I know that well
Ich bin sicher	I'm sure of it
Ich habe (so) eine Ahnung	I've got an idea
Da kenn' ich mich gut aus	I'm very familiar with that
Ich kenne Susi gut	I know Susi well
Wir kennen uns schon	We've met
Ich weiß nicht	I don't know
Ich habe keine Ahnung	I haven't the faintest
Die (den) kenne ich nicht	I don't know her (him)
Da bin ich überfragt!	I can't help you there!

LANGUAGE POINTS
6 Remembering

Weißt du noch, wie ... ? — Do you remember how ... ?
Hast du es dir gemerkt? — Have you remembered it?
Erinnerst du dich an ... ? — Can you remember ... ?
Kannst du dich noch an ... erinnern? — Can you (still) remember ... ?

Sicherlich hast du ... nicht vergessen? — You surely haven't forgotten ... ?
Weißt du nicht mehr? — Have you forgotten?
Erinnerst du dich nicht? — Don't you remember?
Erinnerst du dich nicht an ... ? — Don't you remember ... ?
Ist es dir entfallen? — Has it slipped your memory?
Ich habe nicht vergessen — I haven't forgotten
Ich erinnere mich, ja — I *do* remember
Ich weiß noch, es war im April — I remember it was in April
Daran kann ich mich noch bestimmt erinnern — I can still definitely remember that
Ja, es war so ... — It was like this ...
So weit ich mich entsinne — As far as I can remember

Ich habe es total vergessen! — I've completely forgotten it!
Daran kann ich mich nicht erinnern — I can't remember that
Ich erinnere mich nicht an sie/ihn — I can't remember her/him
Ich weiß nicht mehr! — I don't know anymore!

LANGUAGE POINTS
7 Saying something is true or untrue

Stimmt!	Right!
Das stimmt (doch)!	That's right!
(Das) ist (doch) richtig	(That's) right
Da geb' ich dir recht!	You're right there!
Ganz richtig	Quite right
Das ist wahr	That's true
Das stimmt (gar) nicht!	That's (just) not right!
Das ist gar nicht wahr!	That's just not true!
Das ist gar nicht so!	It's not so at all!
Das gilt nicht immer	That doesn't always hold
Da hast du unrecht!	You're wrong there!
Das ist ganz anders!	It's quite different!

LANGUAGE POINTS
8 Attracting people's attention

Entschuldigung!	
Verzeihung!	Excuse me
Entschuldigen Sie!	
Verzeihen Sie!	
Hier, bitte!	Come here, please: Over here, please
Herr Ober!/Fräulein!	Calling waiter/waitress
Hallo!	Hullo!
Hör mal zu!	Listen!
Seh mal (da)!	Look!
Paß auf!	Watch it! Watch out! Pay attention!

LANGUAGE POINTS
9 Asking someone to do something

Ist das möglich?	Is that possible?
Geht das?	Is that all right?
Ist das in Ordnung?	Is that all right (in order)?
Kannst du . . . ?	Can you . . . ?
Ist das leicht zu erledigen?	Can that be seen to easily?
Kannst du mir . . . besorgen?	Can you see to . . . for me?
Macht das Probleme?	Does that cause problems?
Macht das Schwierigkeiten?	Does that cause difficulties?
Ist das vernünftig?	Is that sensible?

LANGUAGE POINTS
10 Saying you can or can't do something

Keine Sorge!	Don't you worry yourself!
(Das ist) kein Problem!	(That's) no problem!
Das können wir	We can do that
Das geht	That's all right
Das ginge	That's probably all right
Ja, freilich/klar/natürlich/ selbstverständlich/sicher	Yes, of course
Ich glaube nicht	I don't think so
Vermutlich/wahrscheinlich nicht	Probably not
Es tut mir leid, aber . . .	I'm sorry but . . .
Leider nicht	Unfortunately not
Das geht nicht	That can't be done
Unmöglich!	Impossible!
Durchaus nicht!	(in) no way!

LANGUAGE POINTS
11 Asking if something is possible

Könnten wir . . . ?	Could we . . . ?
Glauben Sie, ich könnte . . . ?	Do you think I could . . . ?
Wenn wir . . . gehen?	What about going . . . ?
Wäre es möglich . . . zu gehen?	What about going . . . ?
Wie ist es mit meinem (Taschengeld)?	What about my (pocket money)?
Geht das, . . . ?	Is it all right . . . ?
Kommt sie eventuell?	Is she likely to come?

LANGUAGE POINTS
12 Saying if you think something is possible

Bestimmt	Definitely
Auf jeden Fall	Definitely
Ohne Weiteres	Definitely
Das geht	That's all right/okay/possible
Das ginge	(as above, with slight doubt)
(Das) kann sein	(That) may be
(Das) mag sein	(That) may be
Es ist möglich	It's possible
Es wäre möglich	It would (might) be possible
Das könnte man machen	We could (might) do that
Das ginge nicht	That probably won't work
Das geht nicht	It won't work
Das ist ja unmöglich	It's impossible
Das kommt nicht in Frage!	No question!
Auf keinen Fall!	In no way! / Not at all!
Durchaus nicht!	In no way! / Not at all!
Ausgeschlossen!	Definitely not! / Forget it!

LANGUAGE POINTS
13 Talking about having to do things

Soll ich 'rein kommen? — Should I come it?
Muß ich das (machen)? — Do I have to do that?
Muß ich dann zu Opa gehen? — Do I have to go to grandad's then?
Muß das sein? — Does it have to be?
Ist das unbedingt nötig? — Is that absolutely necessary?
Ist das wirklich notwendig? — Is that really necessary?
Müssen Sie denn hier rauchen? — Do you **have** to smoke here?

Ich darf (nicht) mitkommen — I'm (not) allowed to come
Du sollst dabei sein — You must be there
Ich muß weg! — I've got to go (away)!
Wir müssen das unbedingt schaffen! — We've definitely got to get it done!
Ihr mußt es mal versuchen! — You must just try it!

LANGUAGE POINTS
14 Expressing your wishes

Willst du . . . ? — Do you want to . ?
Wünschen Sie . . . ? — Do you wish to . . . ?
Möchten Sie (gern) . . . ? — Would you like to . . . ?
Wollen wir nicht . . . ? — How about . . . ?
Wie wäre es, wenn wir . . . ? — How would it be, if we . . . ?
Was halten Sie von . . . ? — What do you think to . . . ?
Haben Sie Lust . . . ? — Do you fancy . . . ?

Ich will (nicht) . . . — I (don't) want to . . .
Ich wünsche nicht . . . — I don't wish to . . .
Ich möchte (gern) . . . — I should like . . .
Ich habe keine Lust . . . — I don't fancy . . .
Ich hätte gern ein(e/en) . . . — I should like a . . .
Kann ich, bitte, . . . haben? — May I have . . . ?
Geben Sie mir, bitte, . . . — Please give me . . .
Für mich wäre es . . . — For me it would be . . .
Darf ich, bitte . . . ? — May I . . . ?

LANGUAGE POINTS
15 Making requests

Drei Flaschen Sprudel, bitte! — Three bottles of mineral water, please

Zweimal zweiter Klasse nach Koblenz, hin und zurück, bitte! — Two second class returns to Koblenz, please

Kannst du nicht mit? — Can't you come with us?
Darf ich dir schreiben? — May I write to you?
Darf ich 'rein? — May I come in?
Soll ich anrufen? — Am I to phone?
Ist noch ein Stück Kuchen da? — Is there another piece of cake?
Könnte ich bitte die Illustrierte haben? — Could I have the magazine, please?
Kannst du mir sagen, wie . . . ? — Can you tell me how . . . ?
Wollen wir nicht zusammen essen? — How about eating together?

LANGUAGE POINTS
16 Asking if other people agree or disagree

Einverstanden? — Agreed?
Findest du denn? — Agreed?
Ist sie (nicht) einverstanden? — Does she (not) agree?
Stimmt das, oder? — Is that all right, or what?
Stimmt's oder nicht? — Is that right or not?
Was meinst du? — What do you think?
Wie ist deine Meinung? — What's your opinion?
Bist du auch meiner Meinung? — Do you agree with me?
Sind wir beide derselben Meinung? — Are we of the same opinion?
Hab' ich nicht recht? — Aren't I right?
Wie stehst du (dazu)? — Where do you stand (on it)?
Hast du was dagegen? — Have you (got) anything against it?
Gibst du mir recht? — Do you think I'm right?

LANGUAGE POINTS
17 Telling someone you agree or disagree

(*Das*) *Stimmt!*	Agreed! (with fact)
Einverstanden!	Agreed! (with suggestion)
Ganz richtig	Quite right
Genau	Exactly
Eben	Exactly
Recht hast du	You're right
Du hast recht	You're right
Da gebe ich dir recht	You're right there
Ist richtig	That's right
Das glaube ich auch	I think so, too
Das mein' ich auch	I think so, too
Ich bin derselben Meinung	I'm of the same opinion
Das stimmt (*doch*) *nicht*	I don't agree
Das ist doch total falsch	That's totally wrong
Das ist ja gar nicht wahr	That's just not true
Das kann nicht sein	Can't be
Das glaub' ich nicht	I don't believe that
Das ist Blödsinn/Unsinn/Quatsch!	That's nonsense!
Das ist ganz anders	It's quite different
Ich bin nicht deiner Meinung	I have a different opinion
Da bin ich (*gar*) *nicht einverstanden*	I don't agree (at all) there

LANGUAGE POINTS
18 Giving and asking for help

Kann ich (etwas) helfen?	Can I help?
Wie kann ich helfen?	How can I help?
Soll ich euch helfen?	Shall I help you?
Kann ich dir helfen?	Can I help you?
Was kann ich für Sie tun?	What can I do for you?
Was darf es sein?	What'll it be? / What can I get you?
Suchen Sie etwas?	Are you looking for something?
Was ist denn los?	What's the matter (wrong)?
Wo fehlt's?	Where's the problem? / What's missing?
Hilfe!	Help!
Kannst du mir helfen?	Can you help me?
Ich brauche bitte Hilfe!	I need help, please!
Können Sie mir bitte einen Gefallen tun?	Please can you do me a favour?
Was soll ich tun?	What am I to do?

LANGUAGE POINTS
19 Certainty and doubt

Tatsächlich?	Really?
Tatsache?	Is that a fact?
Ehrlich?	Honestly?
Wirklich?	Really?
Ist das wirklich so?	Is that really so?
Ganz bestimmt?	Is that definite?
Bist du sicher?	Are you sure?
Seid ihr da ganz sicher?	Are you quite sure (of that)?
Weißt du es ganz genau?	Are you quite certain (of it)?
Ohne weiteres	Absolutely
Ganz bestimmt	Quite certain(ly)
Doch bestimmt!	Oh, yes (it is)!
Genau!	Absolutely!
Sicher!	Certainly!/Surely!
Das weiß ich ganz genau!	I'm certain of it!
Das ist Tatsache!	That's a fact!
Da gibt's gar keinen Zweifel!	There's no doubt (of it)!
Darauf können wir uns verlassen!	We can rely on that!
Ich muß es mir mal überlegen	I'll have to think about it
Ich bin nicht hundert Prozent sicher	I'm not a hundred per cent certain
Ich bin nicht überzeugt	I'm not convinced
Das weiß ich (aber) nicht	That I don't know
Ich habe keine Ahnung!	I've no idea!

LANGUAGE POINTS
20 Showing surprise

Wirklich?	Really?
Ist das wahr?	Is that true?
Nicht wahr?	Is that so? (lit. Not true?)
Tatsächlich?	Is that a fact?
Ach, so?	Well! Well!
Na geh!	Get away!
Unglaublich!	Unbelievable!
(Das ist) Kaum zu glauben!	Incredible! (Scarcely credible!)
Unerhört!	Never!

LANGUAGE POINTS
21 Asking about other people's likes

Wie stehst du zu . . . ? — What do you feel about . . . ?
Was sagst du zu . . . ? — What do you think of . . . ?
Wie findest du . . . ? — How do you find (feel about) . . . ?
Was halten sie von . . . ? — What do they think of . . . ?
Haben Sie . . . gern? — Do you like . . . ?
Sagt . . . dir was? — Does . . . mean anything to you?
Ißt du gern . . . ? — Do you like eating . . . ?
Trinken Sie gern . . . ? — Do you like drinking . . . ?
Wie gefällt es dir? — How do you like it?

LANGUAGE POINTS
22 Likes and dislikes

Ausgezeichnet!/Fabelhaft! — Excellent!/Fabulous!
Fantastisch!/Großartig! — Fantastic!/Great!
Toll!/Wunderbar!/Wunderschön! — Smashing!/Wonderful!
Unheimlich gut! — Fantastically good!

Hamburger esse ich (nicht) sehr gern! — I (don't) like hamburgers very much!
Ich mag sie (nicht) — I (don't) like her
Den kann ich (nicht) leiden! — I can(not) stand him!
Gefällt dir Klaus? — Do you like Klaus?
Er gefällt mir (nicht) — I (don't) like him
Wie findest du die Platte? — What do you think of the record?
(Wirklich) Klasse! — (Really) first class!
Das schmeckt (nicht)! — It tastes/doesn't taste good!

Er ärgert sie — He makes her angry
Wir gehen ihr auf die Nerven — We get on her nerves

LANGUAGE POINTS
23 Preferences

Welches hast du lieber? — Which do you prefer?
Welches ziehst du vor? — Which do you prefer?
Ist das dein Lieblings(gericht)? — Is that your favourite (dish)?
Trinkst du lieber Cola oder Bier? — Do you prefer cola or beer?
Essen Sie lieber Eis oder Kuchen? — Do you prefer ice-cream or cake?
Was machst du am liebsten? — What do you like doing best?
Wer gefällt dir am besten? — Whom do you like best?

Ich esse lieber Gemüse als Fleisch — I prefer vegetables to meat
Ich nehme lieber die Bratkartoffeln — I prefer the roast potatoes
Du spielst lieber Hockey — You prefer playing hockey
Dieser gefällt ihm besser — He prefers this one
Ihr wäre es lieber, wenn . . . — She would prefer to . . .
Wir möchten lieber bei dir bleiben — We'd rather stay with you
Ich mag Rugby lieber als Fußball — I prefer rugby to football

Sie machen . . . am liebsten — They like doing . . . best
Am liebsten gehen wir aus — We like going out best

LANGUAGE POINTS
24 Interest and indifference

Interessierst du dich für . . . ? — Are you interested in . . . ?
Haben Sie Interesse für . . . ? — Are you interested in . . . ?
Würde es dich interessieren . . . ? — Would you be interested . . . ?
Ja, ich interessiere mich dafür — Yes, I'm interested in it
Ja, (sehr) gerne — Yes, very much
Ich habe eine Schwäche dafür — I've a weakness for it
Wir begeistern uns fürs Spiel — We're getting enthusiastic about the game

Ich bin begeistert — I'm keen
Ich schwärme für Motorsport — I'm dead keen on motor sport

Das ist mir egal — I can take it or leave it
Mir ist es gleichgültig — I'm indifferent to it

Ich habe kein Interesse dafür — I'm not interested
Wir interessieren uns nicht dafür — We're not interested in it
Das nützt nichts — It's no use

LANGUAGE POINTS
25 Showing satisfaction and dissatisfaction

Nicht so gut	Not so good
Nichts besonders	Nothing special
(Es) Hätte besser sein können	Could have been better
(Es) Geht so	(it's) all right
Nicht so schlecht	Not so bad
Nicht schlecht	Not bad
Vielversprechend	Promising
Ganz gut	Very good
Tadellos	Faultless
Prima (Arbeit)	First class (work)
Hervorragend	Outstanding
(Es) Hätte nicht besser sein können	Couldn't be better

LANGUAGE POINTS
26 Showing you're grateful

Danke!	Thanks! (weak)
Danke schön!	Thank you!
Danke sehr!	Thanks very much!
Danke vielmals!	Many thanks!
Vielen Dank!	Many thanks!
Schönen Dank!	Thanks a lot!
Besten Dank!	Thanks a lot!
Herzlichen Dank!	Thank you very much!
Recht schönen Dank!	Thank you very much indeed
Man dankt!	Thanks! (from a group of people)
Wir danken Ihnen!	We thank you!
Wie kann ich Ihnen danken?	How can I thank you?
Ich bin dir sehr dankbar	I'm very grateful to you
Das war so lieb/nett von dir!	That was so nice of you!
Ich möchte mich bei Ihnen bedanken	I should like to thank you
Wie kann ich mich revanchieren?	How can I repay you! (strong)

LANGUAGE POINTS
27 Congratulating and sympathising

Darf ich gratulieren? — May I congratulate you?
Ich gratuliere — Congratulations
Gut gemacht! — Well done!

Armer Teufel! — Poor devil!
Das tut mir (sehr) leid — I'm (very) sorry about that
Das tut uns (wirklich) leid — We're really sorry
Du (Sie) Ärmste(r) — You poor thing
Herzliches Beileid — All my commiserations/sympathy
Ich fühle mit dir — I feel for you
Ach, wie schade! — Oh, what a pity!
Das ist aber schade! — That's a pity!
Oh je! — Oh dear!
Du Arme(r)! — Poor you!
Pech! — Tough luck!
Du hast Pech! — You're out of luck!
Was für ein Unglück! — What bad luck!
Hoffentlich hast du nächstes Mal mehr Glück! — Better luck next time!
Was für eine Enttäuschung! — What a disappointment!
Da bin ich aber enttäuscht! — That's a disappointment to me!
Sie tun mir aber leid! — I'm sorry for you!
Kann man nichts machen? — Can't anything be done?

LANGUAGE POINTS
28 Showing appreciation or pleasure

Das ist prima! — That's great!
Wie toll! — How nice!
Ich lese sehr gern Krimis! — I really like reading thrillers!
Die Schokolade schmeckt aber gut! — The chocolate tastes good!
Das Sporthemd gefällt mir — I like the sports-shirt
Das freut mich! — I'm really pleased (about it)!
Das macht mir Freude! — That makes me happy!/pleases me!

LANGUAGE POINTS
29 Introducing and meeting new people

Darf ich vorstellen?	May I introduce you?
Darf ich (Uschi) vorstellen?	May I introduce (Uschi)?
Darf ich bekanntmachen?	May I introduce you?
Ich möchte (Susi) vorstellen	I'd like to introduce (Susi)
Hier ist ...	Here is ...
Dies ist ...	This is ...
Kennst du (Benno) schon?	Do you know (Benno)?
Kennt ihr euch schon?	Have you met?
Hallo!	Hullo!
Guten Tag	Good day
Freut mich	Delighted
(Wie) angenehm	Delighted
Macht mir Freude!	It's a pleasure!

LANGUAGE POINTS
30 Making and replying to an apology

Entschuldigung!	Excuse me
Entschuldigen Sie!	Excuse me
Verzeihung!	Excuse me
Verzeihen Sie!	Excuse me
(Es) tut mir leid	Sorry
(Es tut mir sehr leid	I'm very sorry
(Es) tut mir leid, daß ...	I'm sorry that ...
Pardon	Sorry
Bitte (schön)	Please (don't mention it)
(Es) war nichts	It was not important
(Es) macht nichts	It's nothing
(Ist) schon gut	That's all right
Es gibt Schlimmeres	Worse things happen
Das ist gar nicht so schlimm	That's not so bad

LANGUAGE POINTS
31 Worry and fear; warnings

Was ist (mit Ihnen) los? — What's the matter (with you)?
Was fehlt dir? — What's wrong with you?
Was ist? — What's up?
Was geht nicht? — What's not right?
Was haben Sie denn? — What's the matter with you, then?
Hast du Kummer? — Are you worried?
Hast du Sorge? — Are you worried?
Warum hast du Angst? — Why are you worried?
Hast du Angst vor Gespenster? — Are you afraid of ghosts?

Paß auf! — Watch out!/Pay attention!
Nimm dich in acht! — Be careful!
Vorsicht! — Careful!
Seien Sie vorsichtig! — Be careful!
So etwas macht ihm wirklich Sorgen! — Something like that makes him really worry!
Hoffentlich wird das klappen! — Hopefully, it'll come off!
Achtung! — Careful!/Watch out!
Paß auf, daß du nicht sprichst! — Make sure you don't speak!
Nimm dich vor Fremden in acht! — Beware of strangers!
Achte darauf, daß du Geld hast! — Make sure (see to it) that you have money!

LANGUAGE POINTS
32 Greeting people

Guten Tag!	Good day! Good afternoon!
Tag!	Hi
Guten Morgen!	Good morning!
Morgen!	Morning!
Guten Abend!	Good evening!
Abend!	Evening!
Hallo!	Hullo!
Wie geht's?	How's it going?
Mahlzeit!	Hullo! (At mealtimes, passing someone)
Angenehme Ruhe!	Enjoy yourself! (When someone has finished work)
Feierabend!	Enjoy yourself! (as above)
Grüß Gott!	
Grüß dich!	
Grüetzi!	These are all regional ways of saying "Hullo!" in Southern Germany/Austria/Switzerland
Hallihallo!	
Salü!	
Servus!	

LANGUAGE POINTS
33 Saying goodbye

(Auf)Wiedersehen!/Wiederschauen!	Goodbye! (Will see you again!)
Tschüs!	Tata!/Cheerio!
Tschüß	Tata!/Cheerio!
Tschüßchen!	Tata!/Cheerio!
Mahlzeit!	Enjoy your meal!
Gute Nacht!	Good night! (Bed-time)
Mach's gut!	Take care!
Bis morgen!	Until tomorrow!
Bis bald!	See you soon!
Bis dann!	Until then!
Bis später!	Until later!
Bis zum nächsten Mal!	Until (the) next time!
Servus!	So long! (said in Austria/South Germany)
Auf Wiederhören!	Goodbye! (said on phone)

LANGUAGE POINTS
34 Invitations

Samstag ist meine Party	My party is on Saturday
Hast du Lust zu kommen?	Do you fancy coming?
Könnt ihr zu unserer Grillparty kommen?	Can you come to our barbecue?
Hast du Zeit (dazu)?	Have you time?
Paßt dir das?	Does that suit you?
Gehen wir mit?	Shall we go with them?
Gehen wir denn oder nicht?	Are we going or not?
Wenn wir dahin gehen?	What about going there?
Wie wäre es, wenn wir mitspielten?	Shall we play?
Warum denn nicht?	Why not?
Ohne weiteres!	Yes, indeed!
Ja, freilich!	Of course!
Ja, gerne!	Willingly!
Herzlich gern!	With pleasure!
Besten Dank, aber . . .	Thanks a lot, but . . .
Leider kann ich nicht!	Sorry, I can't!
Es geht leider nicht!	It can't be done!

LANGUAGE POINTS
35 Thanking someone and accepting thanks

Danke (schön)	Thank you (very much)
Danke vielmals	Many thanks
Vielen Dank	Many thanks
Schönen Dank	Thanks a lot
Besten Dank	My best thanks
Herzlichen Dank	Very many thanks
Ich möchte mich bedanken	I should like to thank you
Bitte (schön)	Please (don't mention it)
Keine Ursache	It was nothing (There's no reason)
Gern geschehen	It was a pleasure
Nichts zu danken	Nothing to thank me for

LANGUAGE POINTS
36 Asking someone to pass on your good wishes

Schönen Gruß zu Hause! — Say hullo to everybody at home!
Schönen Gruß an deine Schwester! — Best wishes to your sister!
Grüß sie herzlich von mir! — Remember me to them!
Bestell' ihr meine besten Grüße! — Give her my best wishes!
Einen schönen Kuß an Uschi! — Give Uschi a big kiss!

LANGUAGE POINTS
37 Compliments

Deine Jacke paßt dir gut! — Your jacket suits you!
Deine Platte gefällt mir! — I like your record!
Du singst so unheimlich gut! — You sing brilliantly!
Wo(her) hast du das gelernt? — Where did you learn that?

Wirklich? — Really?
Ehrlich? — Honestly?
Sehr nett von dir! — Very nice of you!
Ach, ich weiß nicht! — Oh, I don't know!
Das sagen Sie nur so! — You're only saying that!
Ich tue mein Bestes! — I do my best!
Übung macht den Meister — Practice makes perfect
Ich habe es ja bearbeitet! — I've worked on it!

GERMAN – ENGLISH VOCABULARY

A
ab *from; off*
abbiegen *to turn off*
Abend (m) *evening*
Abendbrot (n);
Abendessen (n) *supper, evening meal*
abends *in the evening(s)*
abfahren *to leave, set off*
Abfahrt (f) *departure*
Abfall (m) *rubbish, refuse*
abfliegen *to take off; fly away*
Abflug (m) *departure (plane)*
abgemacht! *agreed, settled!*
abheben *to take off receiver*
abholen *to fetch, pick up (passenger)*
Abitur (n) *(approx.) A-Level*
ablehnen *to decline, refuse*
abräumen *to clear away/clear the table*
Abs. *sender (back of envelope)*
abschließen *to lock*
Abschlußprüfung (f) *leaving exam*
abschreiben *to copy, crib*
Absender (m) *sender*
abspülen *to wash the dishes*
Abstand halten *to keep your distance*
abstellen *to switch off*
Abteil (n) *compartment*
Abteilung (f) *department*
abtrocknen *to dry*
abwaschen *to wash the dishes*
Achtung (f) *warning, reminder*
ADAC *(equivalent to) AA or RAC*
Adresse (f) *address*
Affe (m) *monkey, ape*
ähnlich *like, similar*
Ahnung (f) *idea, notion*
all- *all, every*
alle sein *to be out (of stock, etc)*
alles Gute *all the best*
allein *alone; but (old fashioned)*
also *so, so then*
alt *old*
Alter (n) *age*
am Apparat *"Speaking!", on the line (phone)*
Amerika *America*
Amerikaner (in) *American (person)*
amerikanisch *American (adj)*
Ampel (f) *traffic light(s)*

an *on (vertical)*
an ... vorbei *past*
an Bord *on board (ship, plane, etc)*
anbieten *to offer*
Andenken (n) *souvenir, reminder*
ander- *other*
anders als *other (than)*
anderthalb *one and a half*
Anfang (m) *beginning*
anfangen *to begin*
angeln *to fish*
Angelrute (f) *fishing rod*
angenehm *pleasant*
Angestellte (m/f) *employee (male, female)*
Angst (f) *fear, anxiety*
anhaben *to have on (clothes)*
per Anhalter fahren *to hitch-hike*
ankommen *to arrive*
Ankunft (f) *arrival*
Anlage (f) *grounds; (wash) rooms*
anlassen *to start engine; leave light on*
Anlieger frei *access for residents*
anmachen *to turn on light/radio, etc*
anmelden (sich) *to book in, register*
Anmeldung (f) *(hotel) reception*
annehmen *to accept*
Anorak (m) *anorak*
anprobieren *to try on*
anrufen *to call, telephone*
Ansager (m) *(radio, tv) announcer, presenter*
anschnallen *to do up (belt)*
Anschrift (f) *address*
ansehen *to watch, look at*
Ansichtskarte (f) *picture postcard*
Antwort (f) *answer*
antworten *to answer*
anziehen *to put on (clothes)*
anziehen (sich) *to get dressed*
Anzug (m) *suit*
Apfel (m) *apple*
Apfelsaft (m) *apple-juice*
Apfelsine (f) *orange*
Apotheke (f) *chemist's*
Apotheker (m) *chemist*
Apparat (m) *set, camera*
April (m) *April*
Arbeit (f) *work*
arbeiten *to work*

144 German–English Vocabulary

Arbeiter (m) *worker*
arbeitislos *unemployed, out of work*
ärgern (sich) *to get angry*
arm *poor*
Arm (m) *arm*
Armband (n) *wrist strap, bracelet*
Armbanduhr (f) *wrist-watch*
Artikel (m) *article*
Arzt (m) *doctor*
Aschenbecher (m) *ashtray*
atemlos *breathless, out of breath*
auch *also*
auf dem Lande *in the country(side)*
auf Deutsch *in German*
auf die Toilette gehen *to go to the toilet(s)*
auf Wiederhören *hope to hear you soon (on phone)*
auf Wiedersehen *goodbye*
aufbauen *to build (up)*
Aufenthalt (m) *stay*
Aufführung (f) *performance, show*
Aufgabe (f) *task, job, exercise*
aufgeben *to give up*
aufhören *to stop, cease*
Aufkleber (m) *sticker*
aufmachen *to open*
Aufnahme (f) *recording*
aufpassen *to pay attention*
aufräumen *to tidy up*
aufschlagen *to (break) open*
Aufschnitt (m) *sliced cold meat*
aufstehen *to stand up*
aufwachen *to wake up*
Aufzug (m) *lift*
Auge (n) *eye*
Augenblick (m) *moment*
August (m) *August*
Aula (f) *assembly hall*
Ausfahrt (f) *exit (motorway, etc)*
ausfallen *to cancel; fall out; turn out (result)*
Ausflug (m) *excursion*
ausfüllen *to fill in (form, etc)*
Ausgang (m) *exit*
ausgeben *to spend*
ausgehen *to go out*
ausgezeichnet *excellent, marvellous*
Auskunft (f) *information*
Ausland (n) *abroad*
Ausländer (m) *foreigner*
ausmachen *to turn off, put out sth*
auspacken *to unpack*
ausreichend *sufficient*

ausruhen (sich) *to have a (good) rest*
ausschalten *to switch off*
aussehen *to look, appear*
außer *except for*
außer Betrieb *out of order*
Aussicht (f) *outlook, view*
aussprechen *to state (a view), express*
aussteigen *to get (climb) out*
Ausstieg (m) *exit (bus, etc)*
austragen *to hold an event*
Austausch (m) *exchange*
Ausverkauf (m) *(clearance) sale*
ausverkauft *sold out*
Auswahl (f) *selection*
Ausweis (m) *pass, identity card*
ausziehen (sich) *to get undressed*
Auto (n) *car*
Autobahn (f) *motorway*
Autobahndreieck (n) *motorway interchange*
Autobahnkreuz (n) *motorway junction*
Autofähre (f) *car-ferry*
Automat (m) *slot vending machine*
Autowäsche (f) *car wash*

B

BRD (f) *the Federal Republic (of Germany)*
Baby (n) *baby*
Bach (m) *stream*
backen *to bake*
Bäcker (m) *baker*
Bäckerei (f) *bakery*
Bad (n) *(swimming) baths*
Badeanzug (m) *swimming costume*
Badehose (f) *swimming trunks*
Bademütze (f) *bathing hat*
baden *to have a bath/swim*
Badetuch (n) *towel*
Badewanne (f) *bath*
Badezimmer (n) *bathroom*
Badminton (n) *badminton*
Bahn (f) *road, track; railway*
Bahnhof (m) *railway station*
Bahnsteig (m) *platform*
bald *soon*
Balkon (m) *balcony; dress circle*
Ball (m) *ball*
Banane (f) *banana*
Bank (f) *bank; bench*
Bart (m) *beard*
basteln *to tinker; do home handicrafts*

German–English Vocabulary 145

Batterie (f) *battery*
Bauch (m) *stomach*
Bauer (m) *farmer*
Bauernhof (m) *farm*
Baum (m) *tree*
Baumwolle (f) *cotton*
Baustelle (f) *building site*
Beamte (m) *official, clerk*
beantworten *to answer*
bedanken (sich) *to thank*
bedeuten *to mean*
bedienen (sich) *to serve o.s.*
Bedienung (f) *service (often 'tip')*
befinden (sich) *to be (situated)*
befriedigend *satisfying, pleasing*
Beginn (m) *beginning*
beginnen *to begin*
begrüßen *to greet*
behandeln *to treat, deal with*
beide *both*
beilegen *to enclose (with letter)*
Bein (n) *leg*
Beispiel (n) *example*
beißen *to bite*
Bekannte (m) *acquaintance*
beklagen (sich) (uber) *to complain (about)*
bekommen *to get*
belegtes Brot *(open) sandwich*
Belgien *Belgium*
Belgier *Belgian (person)*
belgisch *Belgian (adj.)*
beliebt *popular, well-liked*
bellen *to bark*
benutzen *to use; take (train, etc)*
Benzin (n) *petrol*
bequem *comfortable*
Berg (m) *mountain*
Beruf (m) *job, profession*
Berufsberatung (f) *careers guidance*
Berufsschule (f) *further education college*
berufstätig *working (having a job)*
berühmt *famous*
Bescheid wissen *to know about*
beschließen *to decide*
beschreiben *to describe*
Beschreibung (f) *description*
beschweren (sich) *to complain*
besetzt *occupied, taken*
besichtigen *to view, look around*
Besichtigung (f) *visit, viewing (museum, etc)*
besonders *(e)specially*
besorgen *to see to, deal with*

bestehen (auf) *to insist (on)*
bestellen *to order*
bestimmt *definite(ly)*
bestrafen *to punish, fine*
Besuch (m) *visit*
besuchen *to visit*
betreten *to enter, go into; walk on*
Betrieb (m) *factory, business*
Betriebsferien (f) *works holidays*
betrunken *drunk*
Bett (n) *bed*
Bettdecke (f) *blanket, quilt*
Bettwäsche (f) *bedding, bed-linen*
bewegen (sich) *to move*
bewölkt *cloudy, clouded over*
bezahlen *to pay*
Bibliothek (f) *library*
Bier (n) *beer*
bieten *to offer*
Bild (n) *picture*
billig *cheap*
binden *to bind, tie*
Biologie (f) *biology*
Birne (f) *pear; electric bulb*
bis bald *see you soon*
bis gleich *see you very soon*
bis morgen *until tomorrow*
bis nachher *until later (afterwards)*
bis später *until later*
bis zu *up to*
bitte; bitte nochmals *please; don't mention it*
bitte schön *please; here you are*
bitte sehr *please; here you are; don't mention it*
bitten *to ask for*
Blaskapelle (f) *brass band*
blaß *pale*
Blatt (n) *leaf; page of book*
blau *blue*
bleiben *to stay, remain*
Bleistift (m) *pencil*
Blick (m) *look, glance*
blind *blind*
Blitz (m) *lightning*
es blitzt *there's a flash of lightning*
Block (m) *writing pad*
Blockflöte (f) *recorder*
blöd *silly, stupid*
blond *fair (haired)*
Blume (f) *flower*
Blumenkohl (m) *cauliflower*
Bluse (f) *blouse*

146 German–English Vocabulary

Blut (n) *blood*
bluten *to bleed*
Bockwurst (f) *large boiled sausage*
Boden (m) *ground, earth, floor*
Bodensee (m) *Lake Constance*
Bohne (f) *bean*
Bonbon (m) *sweet, candy*
Boot (n) *boat*
böse *nasty, wicked, evil, angry*
braten *to roast, fry*
Brathähnchen (n) *roast/fried chicken*
Bratwurst (f) *fried sausage*
brauchen *to need*
braun *brown*
brechen *to break*
breit *wide*
Bremse (f) *brake*
bremsen *to brake*
Brett (n) *board, plank*
Brief (m) *letter*
Brieffreund (m) *penpal*
Briefkasten (m) *letter-box*
Briefmarke (f) *stamp*
Brieftasche (f) *wallet*
Briefträger (m) *postman*
Briefumschlag (m) *envelope*
Brille (f) *glasses*
bringen *to bring*
Broschüre (f) *brochure, pamphlet*
Brot (n) *bread*
Brötchen (n) *bread roll, sandwich*
Bruder (m) *brother*
Brücke (f) *bridge*
Buch (n) *book*
buchen *to book (in advance)*
buchstabieren *to spell*
bügeln *to iron*
Bühne (f) *stage*
bummeln *to stroll around*
Bundesliga (f) *W. German football league*
Bundesrepublik (f) *the Federal German Republic (West Germany)*
Bungalow (m) *bungalow*
bunt *bright(ly) coloured*
Burg (f) *castle*
Bürgersteig (m) *pavement*
Büro (n) *office*
bürsten (sich) *to brush o.s.*
Bus (m) *bus*
Butter (f) *butter*
Butterbrot (n) *(slice of) bread and butter*
bzw. *and/or*

C

Café (n) *cafe*
Campinggas (n) *bottled gas*
Campingkocher (m) *camp stove*
Campingplatz (m) *camp site*
Celsius *degrees Celsius (centigrade)*
Champignon (m) *(small) mushroom*
Chef (m) *chief, boss; chef*
Chemie (f) *chemistry*
Chips (m.pl.) *(potato) crisps*
cm *centimetres*
Cola (f/n) *coke*
Computer (m) *computer*
Cousin (m) *(male) cousin*
Cousine (f) *(female) cousin*
Currywurst (f) *curried sausage*

D

DB (f) *German Rail*
DDR (f) *German Democratic Republic (East Germany)*
d.h. *i.e. (that is)*
D-Zug (m) *express train*
da *there; as*
Dach (n) *roof*
Dachboden (m) *loft, attic*
damals *then, at that time*
Dame (f) *lady*
Damen (f) *ladies*
Dampfer (m) *steamer*
dankbar *thankful, grateful*
danke *thanks*
danke schön *thank you very much*
danken *to thank*
dann *then*
das geht *that's alright*
Datum (n) *date*
dauern *to last*
Daumen (m) *thumb*
Decke (f) *ceiling; cover; table cloth*
decken *to cover, lay (table)*
denken *to think*
deutsch *German (adj)*
Deutsche (f) *a German woman, girl*
Deutsche Bundesbahn *German Rail*
Deutscher (m) *a German man, boy*
Deutschland (n) *Germany*
Dezember (m) *December*
Dia (n) *photographic slide*
dick *fat*
Dieb (m) *thief*

German–English Vocabulary 147

dienen *to serve*
Dienst (m) *service*
Dienstag (m) *Tuesday*
Diesel (m) *diesel*
Ding (n) *thing*
Dingsda (m, f, n) *thingummibob, what's-his- (her-, its-) name*
direkt *direct, straight through*
Direktor (m) *director, headmaster*
Diskothek *disco*
DM *Deutschmark (German mark)*
doch *yet, however*
Dom (m) *cathedral*
Donau (f) *Danube*
Donner (m) *thunder*
Donnerstag (m) *Thursday*
doof *daft*
Doppelhaus (n) *semi-detached*
Doppelzimmer (n) *double-room*
Dorf (n) *village*
dort *there*
Dose (f) *tin, can, jar, box*
Dosenöffner (m) *tin-opener*
dreckig *dirty, mucky*
Drogerie (f) *drugstore*
Drogist (m) *druggist*
drüben *over there, on the other side*
drücken *to press, squeeze, shake (hands)*
dumm *stupid, silly, not very clever*
dunkel *dark*
dünn *thin*
Durchfall (m) *diarrhoea*
durchfallen *to lose, fail, be a flop*
Durchgangsverkehr (m) *through traffic; goods in transit*
Durst (m) *thirst*
durstig *thirsty*
Dusche (f) *shower*
duschen *to have a shower*
duzen *to call someone 'du'*

E
E111-Schein *E111 form*
echt *genuine*
Ecke (f) *corner*
EG *the EEC*
Ehepaar (n) *married couple*
ehrlich *honest(ly)*
Ei (n) *egg*
eigen *own (adj.)*
Eilzug (n) *semi-fast train*

ein bißchen *a bit, a little*
ein paar *a few*
ein wenig *a little/bit*
Einbahnstraße (f) *one way street*
einfach *simple; single (ticket)*
Einfahrt (f) *entry (on road)*
Einfamilienhaus (n) *detached house*
Eingang (m) *entrance*
einige *some, a few*
einkaufen *to shop*
Einkaufskorb (m) *shopping basket*
Einkaufswagen (m) *shopping trolley*
Einkaufszentrum (n) *shopping centre*
Einkäufe machen *to go shopping*
einladen *to invite*
Einladung (f) *invitation*
einlösen *to cash (cheque)*
einmal *once*
einordnen *to put in order; file*
einpacken *to pack*
einreiben *to rub in*
einreichen *to put in an application*
einschalten *to switch on*
einschenken *to pour*
einschl. *incl.*
einschlafen *to fall asleep*
einschließlich *including*
einsteigen *to get (climb) in*
englisch *English (adj.)*
Enkel (m) *grandson*
Ente (f) *duck*
entschuldigen (sich) *to apologise, say sorry*
Entschuldigung (f) *apology*
entwerten *to cancel (ticket)*
Entwerter (m) *cancelling machine*
Erbse (f) *pea*
Erdbeere (f) *strawberry*
Erdgeschoß (n) *ground floor*
Erdkunde (f) *geography*
erfahren *to experience*
Erfrischungen (f) *refreshments*
Ergebnis (n) *result*
erhalten *receive*
erholen (sich) *to recover*
erinnern (sich) *to remember*
erkältet *to have a cold*
Erkältung (f) *cold (ailment)*
erkennen *to recognise*
erklären *to explain, make clear*
erkundigen (sich) *to enquire*
erlauben *to allow*

148 German–English Vocabulary

Ermäßigung (f) *reduction*
erreichen *to reach*
erste Hilfe *first aid*
erwachen *to awake, arouse*
Einstieg (m) *entrance (bus, etc)*
Eintritt (m) *entrance*
einverstanden *agreed*
einwerfen *to post*
Einwohner (m) *inhabitant*
Einwurf (m) *posting*
Einzelkarte (f) *single ticket*
Einzelzimmer (n) *single room*
Eis (n) *ice, ice cream*
Elefant (m) *elephant*
elektrisch *electric(al)*
Elektro- *electrical (goods, etc)*
Eltern (f) *parents*
Empfang (m) *reception, welcome*
empfehlen *to recommend*
Ende (n) *end*
endlich *finally, in the end*
Endspiel (n) *final (game)*
eng *narrow*
England (n) *England*
Engländer(-in) (m, f) *Englishman, Englishwoman*
Erwachsene *grown-ups, adults*
es gibt *there is/are*
Essen (n) *food, meal*
essen *to eat*
Essig (m) *vinegar*
Eßzimmer (n) *dining room*
Etage (f) *floor, storey*
etwa *about, approximately*
etwas *something*
Europa (n) *Europe*
evangelisch *protestant*

F

Fabrik (f) *factory*
Fach (n) *subject*
Fachhochschule (f) *technical training college*
Fachschule (f) *vocational school*
Fahrausweis (m) *driving licence*
Fähre (f) *ferry*
fahren *to drive, travel (by vehicle)*
Fahrer (m) *driver*
Fahrgast (m) *passenger*
Fahrkarte (f) *ticket*
Fahrplan (m) *time-table*
Fahrpreis (m) *fare*
Fahrrad (n) *cycle*
Fahrschein (m) *driving licence*
Fahrstuhl (m) *lift*
Fahrt (f) *journey*
Fahrzeug (n) *vehicle*
fallen *to fall*
fallen lassen *to drop, let fall*
falls *in case*
falsch *wrong, false*
Familie (f) *family*
Familienname (m) *surname, family name*
Fan (m) *fan*
Fanatiker (m) *fanatic*
fangen *to catch*
Farbe (f) *colour*
fast *almost*
faul *lazy*
Februar (m) *February*
Federball (m) *shuttle; badminton*
Federbett (n) *feather bed*
fehlen *to be missing, lack*
Fehler (m) *mistake*
Feierabend (m) *evening off*
Feiertag (m) *day off*
Feld (n) *field; square (in board game)*
Fenster (n) *window*
Ferien (f) *holidays*
Ferngespräch (n) *phone call*
Fernsehapparat (m) *television set*
fernsehen *to watch television*
Fernseher (m) *television set*
Fernsprecher (m) *telephone*
fertig *ready, finished*
festhalten *to keep hold of s. th.*
feucht *damp, moist*
Feuer haben *to have a light*
Feuerwehr (f) *fire service*
Feuerwehrwagen (m) *fire-engine*
Feuerzeug (n) *cigarette lighter*
Fieber (n) *high temperature, fever*
Film (m) *film*
Filzstift (m) *felt pen*
finden *to find*
Finger (m) *finger*
Firma (f) *firm*
Fisch (m) *fish*
fit *fit, on form*
flach *flat*
Flasche (f) *bottle*
Fleisch (n) *flesh, meat*

German–English Vocabulary

Fleischer (m) *butcher*
Fleischerei (f) *butcher's*
fleißig *hard-working, industrious*
Fliege (f) *fly*
fliegen *to fly*
fließen *to flow*
fließend *fluent(ly)*
Flöte (f) *flute*
Flug (m) *flight*
Flughafen (m) *airport*
Flugzeug (n) *aeroplane*
Flur (m) *hall, corridor, landing*
Fluß (m) *river*
folgen *to follow*
Forelle (f) *trout*
Formular (n) *form*
Forst (m) *forest*
Förster (m) *forester*
Foto (n) *photo*
Fotoapparat (m) *camera*
fotografieren *to photograph*
eine Frage stellen *to ask a question*
fragen *to ask*
Frankreich (n) *France*
Französin (f) *Frenchwoman*
französisch *French (adj.)*
Franzose (m) *Frenchman*
Frau (f) *wife; lady*
Fräulein (n) *young lady, miss*
frei *free; unoccupied*
Freibad (n) *open-air swimming pool*
freihalten *to keep free*
Freitag (m) *Friday*
Freizeit (f) *free time, spare time*
Freizeitsbeschäftigung (f) *hobby, leisure pursuit*
fremd *foreign, strange*
Fremdenzimmer (n) *spare/guest room*
Fremdsprache (f) *foreign language*
fressen *to eat (of animals)*
freuen (sich) *to enjoy o.s.*
Freund (m) *friend*
freundlich *friendly*
frieren *to freeze*
frisch *fresh*
Friseur (m) *hairdresser*
frohe Ostern! *Happy Easter!*
frohe Weihnachten! *Merry Christmas!*
frohes Neujahr! *Happy New Year!*
fröhlich *merry, cheerful*
früh *early*
Frühling (m) *Spring*
Frühstück (n) *breakfast*
frühstücken *to have breakfast*
fühlen (sich) *to feel*
Führerschein (m) *driving licence*
Führung (f) *management*
Füller (m) *fountain-pen*
Fundbüro (n) *lost property office*
furchtbar *fearful*
Fuß (m) *foot*
Fußball (m) *football*
Fußboden (m) *floor*
Fußgänger (m) *pedestrian*
Fußgängerzone (f) *pedestrian precinct*
Futter (n) *animal feed, fodder*
füttern *to feed (animals)*

G
Gabel (f) *fork*
Gang (m) *gait, way of walking*
Gans (f) *goose*
ganz *quite, complete*
Garage (f) *garage*
Garderobe (f) *clothes; cloakroom*
gar nicht *not at all*
Garten (m) *garden*
Gas (n) *gas*
Gast (m) *guest*
Gasthaus (n) *inn*
Gasthof (m) *(country) hotel*
Gaststätte (f) *restaurant*
geb. *née*
Gebäude (n) *building*
geben *to give*
Gebiet (n) *area, region*
Gebirge (n) *mountains*
geboren *born*
gebraten *roast(ed)*
Gebrauchsanweisungen (f) *instructions for use*
Geburtsdatum (n) *date of birth*
Geburtsort (m) *birthplace*
Geburtstag (m) *birthday*
Gebühr (f) *fee, charge*
gebührenpflichtig *subject to a charge*
Gefahr (f) *danger*
gefährlich *dangerous*
Gegend (f) *district, region*
Gegenteil (n) *opposite*
Gehalt (n) *salary*
gehen *to go*
gehören *to belong*
Geige (f) *violin*

150 German–English Vocabulary

gelb *yellow*
Geldstrafe (f) *fine*
gem. *mixed (abbrev.)*
gemischt *mixed*
Gemüse (n) *vegetables*
gemütlich *friendly, snug, cosy*
genau *exact(ly), precise(ly)*
genug *enough, sufficient*
genügen *to be enough, to satisfy*
geöffnet *open(ed)*
Geographie (f) *geography*
Gepäck (n) *luggage*
Gepäckannahme (f) *luggage counter*
Gepäckaufbewahrung (f) *left-luggage office*
Gepäckaufgabe (f) *luggage-counter, baggage check-in*
Gepäckausgabe (f) *baggage checkout*
Gepäcknetz (n) *luggage rack*
Gepäckrückgabe (f) *baggage checkout*
gerade *just, even*
geradeaus *straight on*
Gericht (n) *court (of law)*
gern *willingly*
gern haben *to like*
Gesamtschule (f) *comprehensive school*
Geschäft (n) *business, shop*
Geschäftsmann (m) *business man*
Geschäftszeiten (f) *business hours*
Geschenk (n) *present*
Geschichte (f) *story, history*
geschieden *divorced*
Geschirr (n) *crockery*
Geschlecht (n) *sex, gender*
geschlossen *closed*
Geschwister (n) *brother(s) and sister(s)*
Geschwindigkeit (f) *speed*
Gesicht (n) *face*
gesperrt *closed, barred*
Gespräch (n) *conversation*
gestattet *allowed, permitted*
gestern *yesterday*
gestrichen *painted*
gesund *healthy*
Getränk (n) *drink*
Getränkekarte (f) *wine-list*
gewinnen *to win*
Gewitter (n) *thunder storm*
gewöhnlich *usually*
Gipfel (m) *top, summit*
Gips (m) *plaster of Paris*
Gitarre (f) *guitar*

Glas (n) *glass*
glauben *to believe*
gleich *like, similar, same*
gleichfalls *the same (to you)*
Gleis (n) *platform, line, track*
glücklich *happy, fortunate*
Gold (n) *gold*
Goldfisch (m) *goldfish*
Gottesdienst (m) *(Church) service*
Grad (m) *degree*
Gramm (n) *gramme*
Gras (n) *grass*
gratulieren *to congratulate*
grau *grey*
Grenze (f) *border*
grillen *to grill, barbecue*
Grippe (f) *flu*
Groschen (f) *Groschen (Austr. currency); 10 Pfennigs*
Größe (f) *size*
groß *big*
Grundschule (f) *primary school*
Gruppe (f) *group*
Gruß (m) *greeting*
grün *green*
grüne Karte *green card*
Grüß Gott! *Good day! (S. Germany and Austria)*
grüßen *to greet*
gucken *to look*
Gulasch (n) *goulash*
gültig *valid*
Gummi (m/n) *rubber, eraser*
günstig *convenient, favourable*
Gurke (f) *cucumber*
Gürtel (m) *belt*
gut *good, well*
gut gelaunt *in a good mood*
gute Besserung! *Speedy recovery!*
gute Fahrt! *Safe journey!*
gute Heimfahrt *Safe return!*
gute Nacht! *Good night!*
gute Reise! *Pleasant journey!*
guten Abend! *Good evening!*
guten Appetit! *Enjoy your meal!*
guten Morgen! *Good morning!*
guten Tag! *Good day!*
Gymnasium (n) *grammar school*

H

Haar (n) *hair*
Haarbürste (f) *hairbrush*

German–English Vocabulary 151

Haarshampoo (m) *(hair) shampoo*
Haarwaschmittel (n) *shampoo*
haben *to have*
Hafen (m) *harbour, port*
Hagel (m) *hail*
hageln *to hail*
Hähnchen (m) *chicken*
halb *half, semi (adj., adv.)*
Halbpension (f) *half-board*
Hälfte (f) *half*
Hallenbad (m) *indoor swimming pool*
Hallo! *Hullo!*
Hals (m) *neck*
halten *to hold*
Haltestelle (f) *(bus, etc) stop*
Hamster (m) *hamster*
Hand (f) *hand*
Handarbeit (f) *handicraft; manual work*
Handball (m) *handball*
Handlung (f) *shop, business*
Handschuh (m) *glove*
Handtasche (f) *handbag*
Handtuch (m) *towel*
häßlich *ugly, hateful*
Hauptbahnhof (m) *(main) railway station*
Hauptschule (f) *general secondary school*
Hauptstraße (f) *main street*
Haus (n) *house*
Hausaufgaben (f) *homework*
Hausfrau (f) *housewife*
Haushalt (m) *household*
Hausmeister (m) *caretaker, janitor*
Hausnummer (f) *house number*
Haustier (n) *pet*
Heft (n) *exercise book; number (periodical)*
Heftpflaster (n) *sticking plaster*
Heilig Abend (m) *Christmas Eve*
Heimat (f) *home*
Heimweh haben *to be homesick*
heiraten *to marry*
heiß *hot*
heißen *to be called; to mean*
heiter *cheerful*
heizen *to heat*
Heizung (f) *heating*
helfen *to help*
hell *bright; light (adj.)*
Hemd (n) *shirt*
Herbergsmutter (f) *hostel warden (female)*
Herbergsvater (m) *hostel warden (male)*
Herbst (m) *Autumn*

Herd (m) *oven, cooker*
herein *in*
Herr (m) *gentleman; sir*
Herr Ober! (m) *Waiter!*
Herren (m. pl.) *gentlemen*
Herrenkonfektion (f) *men's clothing/suit*
Herrenmode (f) *men's fashion*
herrlich *magnificent*
Herz (n) *heart*
herzliche Grüße! *Hearty greetings!*
herzlichen Glückwunsch *Hearty good wishes!*
heute *today*
hier *here*
Hilfe (f) *help (see also Erste Hilfe)*
Himbeere (f) *raspberry*
Himmel (m) *sky; heaven*
hin und zurück *there and back, return*
hinauslehnen *to lean out*
hinlegen (sich) *to lie down*
hinsetzen (sich) *to sit down*
hinten *behind*
Hitparade (f) *hit parade*
Hitze (f) *heat*
Hobby (n) *hobby*
hoch *high*
hochachtungsvoll *yours very sincerely/respectfully*
Hochhaus (n) *tower block*
Hochsprung (m) *high jump*
Höchstgeschwindigkeit (f) *top speed*
Höchsttemperatur (f) *highest temperature*
Hof (m) *farm; yard*
hoffen *to hope*
hoffentlich *hopefully*
holen *to fetch*
Holland (n) *Holland*
Holländer(-in) (m, f) *Dutchman, Dutchwoman*
holländisch *Dutch*
Holz (n) *wood*
Honig (m) *honey*
hören *to hear*
Hörer *listener; receiver (radio/phone)*
Hose (f) *trousers*
Hotel (n) *hotel*
Hubschrauber (m) *helicopter*
hübsch *pretty*
Hügel (m) *hill*
Huhn (n) *chicken, hen*
Hund (m) *dog*
Hunger (m) *hunger*

German–English Vocabulary

hungrig *hungry*
husten *to cough*
Hut (m) *hat*
Hütte (f) *hut*

I

Idee (f) *idea*
Illustrierte (f) *(illustrated) magazine*
im Freien *in the open air/countryside*
Imbiß (m) *snack, light meal*
Imbißstube (f) *snack bar*
immer (noch) *still, always*
inbegriffen *included*
Industrie (f) *industry*
Ingenieur (m) *engineer*
inklusive *inclusive*
Inland (n) *home country*
Insekt (n) *insect*
Insel (f) *island*
Instrument (n) *instrument*
intelligent *intelligent*
Inter-City-Zug (m) *inter-city train*
interessant *interesting*
Interesse (n) *interest*
interessieren (sich—für) *to be interested (in)*
irgendwo *somewhere or other*
Italien (n) *Italy*
Italiener(-in) (m/f) *Italian man, Italian women*
italenisch *Italian*

J

ja *yes*
Jacke (f) *jacket*
Jahr (n) *year*
Jahreszeit (f) *season*
Jahrhundert (n) *century*
jährlich *yearly*
Januar (m) *January*
Jeans (f) *Jeans*
Jeansstoff (m) *denim*
jetzt *now*
Job (m) *job*
joggen *to go jogging*
Jogging (n) *jogging*
Joghurt (m/n) *yoghurt*
Jugendclub (m) *youth club*
Jugendherberge (f) *youth hostel*
Jugendliche (f) *young person, youth (female)*
Jungendlicher (m) *young person, youth (male)*
Juli (m) *July*
jung *young*
Junge (m) *boy, lad*
Juni (m) *June*

K

Kaffee (m) *coffee*
Kaffeekanne (f) *coffee pot*
Käfig (m) *cage*
Kakao (m) *cocoa*
Kalbfleisch (n) *veal*
kalt *cold (adj.)*
Kälte (f) *the cold*
kalte Platte (f) *cold dish*
Kamm (m) *comb*
kämmen (sich) *to comb o.s.*
Kanal (m) *the Channel*
Kanalinseln (pl) *Channel Islands*
Kaninchen (n) *rabbit*
Ännchen (n) *small pot*
Kapelle (f) *band*
kapieren *to understand, get it*
kaputt *broken, gone wrong*
Karte (f) *card, ticket*
Kartoffel (f) *potato*
Kartoffelbrei (m) *mashed potato*
Kartoffelsalat (m) *potato salad*
Käse (m) *cheese*
Kasse (f) *checkout, cash-desk*
Kassenzettel (m) *sales receipt*
Kassette (f) *cassette*
Kassettenrekorder (m) *cassette recorder*
Kater (m) *tomcat*
Kater haben *to have a hangover*
katholisch *catholic*
Katze (f) *cat*
kauen *chew*
kaufen *to buy*
Kaufhaus (n) *department store*
Kaufmann (m) *tradesman, dealer, business man*
Kaugummi (m) *chewing gum*
kegeln *to bowl (10-pin, etc)*
Keks (m) *biscuit*
Keller (m) *cellar*
Kellner(-in) (m, f) *waiter, waitress*
kennen *to know*
kennenlernen *to get to know*
Kerze (f) *candle*
Kette (f) *chain*

German–English Vocabulary

Kilo (n) *kilo*
Kilometer (n) *kilometre*
Kind (n) *child*
Kindergarten (m) *kindergarten, nursery school*
Kinderteller (m) *child's plate (in restaurant, etc)*
kinderleicht *child's play*
Kino (n) *cinema*
Kiosk (m) *kiosk*
Kirche (f) *church*
Kirmes (f) *(annual) village fair*
Kirsche (f) *cherry*
Kissen (n) *cushion, pillow*
klappbar *folding*
klappen *to fold; come off (to be successful)*
Klappstuhl (m) *folding chair*
Klapptisch (m) *folding table*
klar *clear, obvious*
klasse *great, first class*
Klasse (f) *class*
Klassenarbeit (f) *classwork*
Klassenbuch (f) *class book, text book*
Klassenfahrt (f) *class trip*
Klassenlehrer(-in) (m/f) *class teacher*
Klassensprecher(-in) (m/f) *form captain*
Klassenzimmer (n) *classroom*
klassisch *classic(al)*
klauen *to swipe, pinch, crib*
Klavier (n) *piano*
kleben *to stick*
Kleid (n) *dress*
Kleider (f) *clothes*
Kleiderschrank (m) *wardrobe*
klein *little, small*
Kleingeld (n) *change (money)*
klettern *to climb, clamber*
Klima (n) *climate*
klingeln *to ring*
Klinik (f) *clinic, teaching hospital*
Klo (n) *loo*
klopfen *to knock*
Klub (m) *club*
Kneipe (f) *bar, pub*
Knie (m) *knee*
knipsen *to punch (a ticket); flick (a switch)*
Knödel (m) *dumpling*
Knopf (m) *button, switch*
kochen *to cook, boil*
Koffer (m) *case*
Kofferkuli (m) *luggage trolley*
Kofferraum (m) *(car) boot*

Kohle (f) *coal*
komisch *funny, peculiar*
kommen *to come*
Komödie (f) *comedy*
kompliziert *complicated*
Kompott (n) *stewed fruit*
Konditorei (f) *confectionery and cake shop*
kontrollieren *to check (passports, etc)*
Konzert (n) *concert*
Kopf (m) *head*
Kopfkissen (n) *pillow*
Körper (m) *body*
körperbehindert *disabled*
korrigieren *to correct*
kostbar *precious*
kosten *to cost*
kostenlos *free of charge*
Kostüm (n) *costume; lady's suit*
Kotelett (n) *chop, cutlet*
krank *ill, sick*
Krankenhaus (n) *hospital*
Krankenkasse (f) *health insurance scheme*
Krankenschein (m) *certificate entitling patient to treatment*
Krankenschwester (f) *nurse*
Krankenwagen (m) *ambulance*
Krawatte (f) *tie*
Kreide (f) *chalk*
Kreis (m) *circle, district*
kriegen *to get*
Krimi (m) *whodunnit*
Küche (f) *kitchen*
Kuchen (m) *cake*
Kuckucksuhr (f) *cuckoo clock*
Kugelschreiber (m) *ballpoint pen*
Kuh (f) *cow*
kühl *cool*
Kühlschrank (m) *fridge*
Kuli (m) *ballpoint pen; trolley*
Kunst (f) *art*
Kunststoff (m) *plastic*
Kur (f) *treatment*
Kurort (m) *health resort, spa*
Kurs (m) *rate of exchange*
kurz *short*
Kusine (f) *cousin (female)*
Küste (f) *coast*

L
Labor (n) *laboratory*
lachen *to laugh*

German–English Vocabulary

Laden (m) *shop*
Lage (f) *place, situation*
Lampe (f) *lamp*
Land (n) *land, country(side); large admin. region*
landen *to land*
Landkarte (f) *map*
Landschaft (f) *landscape, scenery*
lang *long*
lange *a long time*
langsam *slow(ly)*
Langspielplatte (f) *L.P.*
langweilig *boring*
Lappen (m) *rag, cloth*
Lärm (m) *(loud) noise*
lassen *to leave, let*
Latein (n) *Latin*
laufen *to run*
laut *loud*
läuten *to ring*
Leben (n) *life*
Lebensgefahr (f) *danger to life*
Lebensmittel (pl) *food*
Lebensmittelgeschäft (n) *food shop*
Leberwurst (f) *liver sausage*
lecker *tasty*
Leder (n) *leather*
ledig *unmarried, single*
leer *empty*
Leerung (f) *(post) collection*
legen *to lay*
Lehrer(-in) (m/f) *teacher*
Lehrling (m) *apprentice, trainee*
leicht *easy*
Leichtathletik (f) *athletics (track and field)*
leider *unfortunately*
leihen *to lend*
leise *gently, quietly*
Leistung (f) *achievement, performance*
lernen *to learn*
lesen *to read*
letzt *last*
Leute (f) *people*
Licht (n) *light*
liebe Hanna *Dear Hanna*
lieben *to love, like very much*
lieber Uli *Dear Uli*
Lieblingsfach (n) *favourite subject*
liefern *to deliver*
Lieferwagen (m) *delivery van*
liegen *to lie*
Liegewagen (m) *couchette car (on train)*
Lift (m) *lift*
Limonade (f) *lemonade, fizzy drink*
Lineal (n) *ruler*
Linie (f) *line, bus number (route)*
links *left*
Liste (f) *list*
Liter (m/n) *litre*
Lkw (m) *HGV*
loben *to praise*
Löffel (m) *spoon*
Lohn (m) *wages, salary*
lösen *to buy (ticket)*
Löwe (m) *lion, Leo (star-sign)*
Luft (f) *air*
Luftmatratze (f) *airbed*
Luftpost (f) *airmail*
Lust (f) *desire, fancy, inclination*
Lust haben *to fancy*
lustig *merry*

M
machen *to do, make*
Mädchen (n) *girl*
Mädchenname (m) *girl's name*
Magazin (n) *magazine*
Magen (m) *stomach*
Mahlzeit (f) *mealtime; enjoy your meal*
Mai (m) *May*
mal *time(s); just*
Mal (n) *time*
malen *to paint*
manchmal *sometimes*
mangelhaft *defective, faulty*
Mann (m) *man, husband*
männlich *manly, masculine*
Mannschaft (f) *team*
Mantel (m) *coat*
Mappe (f) *satchel, briefcase*
Margarine (f) *margarine*
Mark (f) *Mark (coin)*
Markstück (n) *one Mark coin*
Markt (m) *market*
Marktplatz (m) *market square*
Marmelade (f) *jam*
März (m) *March*
Maschine (f) *machine*
Mathe (f) *maths*
Mathematik (f) *mathematics*
Medizin (f) *medicine*
Meer (n) *sea*
Meerschweinchen (n) *guinea pig*

German–English Vocabulary 155

mehr *more*
Mehrfahrtenkarte (f) *saver-ticket, saver-strip*
Mehrwertsteuer (f) *V.A.T.*
Meile (f) *mile*
meinen (f) *to mean*
melden *to report, register*
Menge (f) *amount, quantity; loads of*
Mensch (m) *human being*
Menü (n) *menu*
Messe (f) *mass (church); (trade) fair*
Messer (n) *knife*
Meter (n) *metre*
Metzger (m) *butcher*
Metzgerei (f) *butcher's shop*
mieten *to rent, hire*
Milch *milk*
mild *mild*
Mineralwasser (n) *mineral water*
Minute (f) *minute*
mir *to (for) me*
Mißverständnis (n) *misunderstanding*
mitbringen *to bring with you*
Mitglied (m) *member*
mitkommen *to come with s.o.*
mitnehmen *to take with s.o.*
Mittag (m) *midday*
Mittagessen (n) *midday meal*
Mittagspause (f) *midday break*
Mitte (f) *middle*
Mittelmeer (n) *Mediterranean (sea)*
mitten in *in the middle of*
Mitternacht (f) *midnight*
Mittwoch (m) *Wednesday*
Möbel (n) *(item of) furniture*
möbliert *furnished*
Mode (f) *fashion*
modern *modern*
Mofa (n) *moped*
mogeln *to cheat*
möglich *possible, likely*
Moment (m) *moment*
Monat (m) *month*
monatlich *monthly*
Mond (m) *moon*
Montag (m) *Monday*
morgen *tomorrow*
Morgen (m) *morning*
morgens *in the morning(s)*
Motor (m) *engine*
Motorrad (n) *motor-bike*
Mund (m) *mouth*

müde *tired*
mündlich *oral*
Münze (f) *coin*
Münzwäscher (m) *launderette, coin-op*
Museum (n) *museum*
Musik (f) *music*
Mutter (f) *mother*
Mutti (f) *mummy*
München (n) *Munich*
Mütze (f) *(woolly) cap*

N

nach *after; to(wards)*
Nachbar(-in (m, f) *neighbour (male, female)*
nachgehen *to follow*
nachher *afterwards*
Nachmittag (m) *afternoon*
nachmittags *in the afternoon(s)*
Nachname (m) *surname, family name*
Nachrichten (f) *news*
nachsehen *to look into, check up*
nachsitzen *to be kept in, detained (school)*
Nachspeise (f) *dessert, sweet*
nächst *next (to)*
Nacht (f) *night*
Nachtisch (m) *dessert, sweet*
nachts *in the night(s)*
Nachttisch (m) *bedside table*
in der Nähe *near(by)*
nähen *to sew*
Nahverkehrszug (m) *local train*
Name (m) *name*
Namenstag (m) *name-day*
Nase (f) *nose*
Nässe (f) *wet(ness)*
naß *wet*
Natur (f) *nature*
natürlich *natural(ly)*
Nebel (m) *fog*
Nebenstraße (f) *side-street*
neblig *foggy*
Neffe (m) *nephew*
nehmen *to take*
nein *no*
nennen *to call*
nervös *nervous, nervy*
nett *nice*
Netz (n) *net*
neu *new*
neugierig *curious*
Neujahr (n) *New Year*

nicht *not*
nicht mehr *no more*
nicht wahr *not true*
Nichte (f) *niece*
Nichtraucher (m) *non-smoker*
nichts *nothing*
nichts zu danken *don't mention it*
nie *never*
Niederlande (f) *Netherlands*
Niederschlag (m) *rainfall*
niesen *to sneeze*
noch *still*
noch einmal *once more*
noch nicht *not yet*
Nord (m) *north*
Nordsee (f) *North Sea*
normal *normal, ordinary*
Notausgang (m) *emergency exit*
Notdienst (m) *emergency service*
Note (f) *(school) mark; note*
Notruf (m) *emergency call*
November (m) *November*
null *nought, zero*
Nummer (f) *number*
nun *now*
nur *only*

O
oben *above, upstairs*
Oberstufe (f) *6th Form, upper school*
Obst (n) *fruit*
Ofen (m) *oven*
offen *open*
öffnen *to open*
Öffnungszeiten (f) *opening times*
oft *often*
Ohr (n) *ear*
Oktober (m) *October*
Öl (n) *oil*
Oma (f) *granny*
Omelett (n) *omelette*
Onkel (m) *uncle*
Opa (m) *grandad*
Orange (f) *orange*
Orangensaft (m) *orange-juice*
Orchester (n) *orchestra*
Ordnung (f) *order*
organisieren *to organise*
Ort (m) *place*
Ortsgespräch (n) *local phone call*
Ost (m) *east*
Ostern *Easter*
Österreich (n) *Austria*
Österreicher(-in) (m/f) *Austrian (male, female)*
österreichisch *Austrian (adj.)*
Ostsee (f) *Baltic*

P
(ein) paar *a few*
Paar (n) *pair*
packen *to pack*
Päckchen (n) *pack (cigarettes, etc), small packet/parcel*
Paket (n) *parcel*
paniert *[cooked] in breadcrumbs*
Panne (f) *breakdown*
Papier (n) *paper*
Papiere (f) *papers, documents*
Park (m) *park; parking*
parken *to park*
Parkett (n) *stalls (cinema, theatre seats)*
Parkhaus (n) *multi-storey car park*
Parkplatz (m) *parking place*
Parkschein (m) *parking ticket*
Parkuhr (f) *parking meter*
Parkverbot (n) *parking ban*
Paß (m) *passport, identity card*
Passagier (m) *passenger*
passen *to fit, match*
passieren *to happen; to pass (by)*
Paßkontrolle (f) *Passport Control*
Patient(-in) (m/f) *patient*
Pause (f) *pause, break*
Pech (n) *bad luck*
Pension (f) *boarding house; full-board*
per Anhalter fahren *to hitch-hike*
Personn (f) *person*
Pfadfinder (m) *scout*
Pfeffer (m) *pepper*
Pfeife (f) *pipe*
Pfennig (m) *pfennig*
Pferd (n) *horse*
Pfingsten *Whitsun*
Pfirsich (m) *peach*
Pflanze (f) *plant*
Pflaster (n) *sticking plaster; pavement*
Pflaume (f) *plum*
Pflichtfach (n) *compulsory subject*
Pfund (n) *pound*
Physik (f) *physics*
Picknick (n) *picnic*
Pille (f) *pill*
Pils (n) *Pilsener beer*

German–English Vocabulary

Pilz (m) *mushroom; toadstool*
Pkw (m) *passenger car*
planmäßig *scheduled, planned*
Plastik (n) *plastic*
Platte (f) *record*
Plattenspieler (m) *record player*
Platz (m) *place*
Platz nehmen *to take one's place*
plaudern *to chat*
plötzlich *suddenly*
Pokal (m) *sports cup, goblet*
Polizei (f) *police*
Poliziewache (f) *police-station*
Polizist(-in) (m, f) *policeman, policewoman*)
Pommes frites *chips*
Popmusik (f) *pop music*
Portemonnaie (n) *purse*
Portion (f) *helping, portion*
Post (f) *post*
Postamt (n) *post-office*
Poster (n) *poster*
Postkarte (f) *postcard*
Postleitzahl (f) *post-code (zip-code)*
Postwertzeichen (n) *postage stamp*
Praline (f) *(individual) chocolate*
Preis (m) *price*
preiswert *reasonably priced, good value*
prima *first class, great*
pro *per*
probieren *to try, test*
Problem (n) *problem*
Profi (m) *pro(fessional)*
Programm (n) *programme*
Prospekt (m) *brochure, leaflet*
Prost/Prosit (n) *toast (drink), cheers!*
prüfen *to test, examine*
Prüfung (f) *test, examination*
Pudding (m) *(similar to) blancmange*
Pulli (m) *pullover, sweater*
Pullover (m) *pullover, sweater*
Pult (n) *(school) desk*
Punkt (m) *point*
pünktlich *punctual*
Puppe (f) *doll*
putzen *to polish, clean*

Q
Qualität (f) *quality*
Quatsch (m) *rubbish, nonsense*
Querstraße (f) *street crossing another*

Quittung (f) *bill, receipt*

R
R-Gespräch (n) *reverse charges call*
Rad (n) *wheel, bike*
radfahren *to cycle*
Radfahrer (m) *cyclist*
Radiergummi (m/n) *eraser, rubber*
Radio (n) *radio*
Rang (m) *row (in cinema, etc)*
Rasen (m) *turf, lawn*
Rasierapparat (m) *shaver*
rasieren (sich) *to shave o.s.*
Rasthof (m) *motel*
Rastplatz (m) *lay-by, pull-in*
Raststätte (f) *(motorway) service area*
raten *to advise*
Rathaus (n) *town hall*
rauchen *to smoke*
Raucher (m) *smoker*
Raum (m) *room; space*
Realschule (f) *secondary modern school*
rechnen *to count (up)*
Rechnung (f) *bill*
Recht haben *to be right*
rechts *right*
reden *to speak, talk*
Regal (n) *shelves, book-shelves, book-case*
Regen (m) *rain*
Regenmantel (m) *raincoat*
Regenschirm (m) *umbrella*
regnen *to rain*
regnerisch *rainy*
reiben *to rub, grate; grind (coffee)*
reich *rich*
reichen *to reach; be enough*
Reifen (m) *tyre*
Reifendruck (m) *tyre-pressure*
Reifenpanne (f) *flat tyre*
Reihe (f) *row; turn*
Reihenhaus (n) *terraced house*
Reinigung (f) *cleaning, cleaners*
Reis (m) *rice*
Reise (f) *journey*
Reiseandenken (n) *souvenir*
Reiseauskunft (f) *travel information*
Reisebüro (n) *travel agency*
Reisefuhrer(-in) (m, f) *guide*
Reiseleiter(-in) (m, f) *tour leader*
reisen *to travel*
Reisende (m, f) *traveller*
Reisescheck (m) *traveller's cheque*

German–English Vocabulary

reiten *to ride*
Reklame (f) *(large) advert, poster, publicity*
Religion (f) *religion*
rennen *to run*
Rentner(-in) (m, f) *pensioner*
Reparatur (f) *repair*
Reparaturwerkstatt (f) *repair workshop*
reparieren *to repair*
reservieren *to reserve*
Restaurant (n) *restaurant*
retten *to save, rescue*
Rezept (n) *prescription*
Rhein (m) *the Rhine*
richtig *richtig*
Richtung (f) *direction*
riechen (nach) *to smell of*
Rindfleisch (n) *beef*
Ring (m) *ring, circle*
Rock (m) *skirt*
Roller (m) *scooter (motor or child's)*
Rollschuh (m) *roller-skate*
Rolltreppe (f) *escalator*
Roman (m) *novel*
rosa *pink*
rot *red*
Rotwein (m) *red wine*
Rücken (m) *back*
Rückfahrkarte (f) *return ticket*
Rückgabe (f) *return (luggage, etc)*
Rucksack (m) *rucksack*
Ruderboot (n) *rowing boat*
rudern *to row*
rufen *to call*
Ruhe (f) *rest; peace, quiet*
Ruhetag (m) *rest-day*
ruhig *peaceful, quiet*
Rührei (n) *scrambled eggs*
rund *round*
Rundfahrt (f) *circular tour*
Rundfunk (m) *radio*

S

Sack (m) *sack, large bag*
Sackgasse (f) *cul-de-sac*
S-bahn (f) *urban railway*
Saal (m) *hall, large room*
Sache (f) *thing*
Saft (m) *juice*
sagen *to say, tell*
Sahne (f) *cream*
Saison (f) *season*
Salat (m) *lettuce*
Salz (n) *salt*
Salzkartoffel (f) *boiled potato*
sammeln *to collect*
Sammlung (f) *collection*
Samstag (m) *Saturday*
Sand (m) *sand*
Sandale (f) *sandal*
Sänger(-in) (m, f) *singer*
satt *enough*
sauber *clean*
sauber machen *to clean*
sauer *sour*
Sauerkraut (n) *sauerkraut*
Sauwetter (n) *filthy weather*
sb-tanken *serve-yourself (petrol)*
Schach (n) *chess*
Schachtel (f) *box, packet*
schade *a shame*
Schaf (n) *sheep*
Schaffner (m) *conductor, ticket inspector*
Schal (m) *scarf*
Schale (f) *skin, peel, shell*
Schallplatte (f) *record*
Schalter (m) *ticket window*
scharf *sharp*
Schatten (m) *shadow*
schauen *to look, see*
Schauer (m) *shower (rain)*
Schaufenster (n) *(shop) display window*
Schauspiel (n) *play, drama*
Schauspieler(-in) (m, f) *actor, actress*
schälen *to peel*
Scheck (m) *cheque*
Scheckkarte (f) *cheque card*
Scheibe (f) *window pane, windscreen*
Schein (m) *banknote, licence*
scheinen *to seem, appear*
Scheinwerfer (m) *headlamp, searchlight*
schellen *to ring*
Schenke (f) *tavern*
schicken *to send*
schießen *to shoot*
Schiff (n) *ship*
Schild (n) *sign; shield*
Schildkröte (f) *tortoise*
Schilling (m) *schilling (Austrian currency)*
schlafen *to sleep*
Schlafsack (m) *sleeping bag*
Schlafwagen (m) *sleeper (train, coach)*
Schlafzimmer (n) *bedroom*
Schlager (m) *pop song; hit*

schlagen *to hit, beat*
Schlagsahne (m) *whipped cream*
Schlagzeug (n) *drums*
Schläger (m) *drummer*
Schlange (f) *snake*
schlank *slender, slim*
schlecht *bad*
schlecht gelaunt *in a bad mood*
schließen *to shut, close*
Schließfach (n) *(luggage) locker, PO Box*
schließlich *finally, eventually*
schlimm *bad*
Schlips (m) *tie*
Schlittschuh (m) *skate*
Schloß (n) *castle; lock*
schlucken *to swallow*
Schluß machen *to finish*
Schlüssel (m) *key*
schmal *narrow*
schmecken *to taste*
schmerzen *to hurt, pain*
Schmuck (m) *decoration, jewellery*
schmutzig *dirty*
Schnaps (m) *schnaps, liqueur*
Schnee (m) *snow*
schneiden *to cut*
schneien *to snow*
schnell *fast, quick(ly)*
Schnellimbiß (m) *snack bar, fast-food outlet*
Schnellreinigung (f) *(express) dry-cleaners*
Schnellzug (m) *fast train*
Schnitzel (n) *escalope*
Schnupfen (m) *head cold*
Schnurrbart (m) *moustache*
Schokolade (f) *chocolate*
schon *already*
schön *nice, beautiful*
Schrank (m) *cupboard*
schrecklich *awful, frightful*
schreiben *to write*
Schreibmaschine (f) *typewriter*
Schreibpapier (m) *writing paper*
Schreibwarenhandlung (f) *stationer's*
Schreibwarenhändler(-in) (m, f) *stationer*
schriftlich *written*
Schritt fahren *to drive dead slow*
Schuh (m) *shoe*
Schulbuch (n) *schoolbook*
Schule (f) *school*
Schüler(-in) (m, f) *pupil, scholar*

German–English Vocabulary 159

Schülerlotse (m) *school traffic-warden*
schulfrei *no school*
Schulhof (m) *school yard*
Schultasche (f) *satchel*
Schulter (f) *shoulder*
Schüssel (f) *bowl, dish*
schützen *to score (goal, etc); protect*
schwach *weak*
Schwager (m) *brother-in-law*
Schwamm (m) *sponge*
schwänzen *to play truant*
schwarz *black*
schwarz fahren *to travel without a ticket; drive without a licence*
schwarze Brett (n) *notice board*
Schwein (n) *pig*
Schweinefleisch (n) *pork*
Schweiz (f) *Switzerland*
Schweizer(-in) (m, f) *Swiss (man, woman)*
schweizerisch *Swiss (adj.)*
schwer *heavy*
Schwester (f) *sister*
Schwieger— —*-in-law*
schwierig *difficult*
Schwimmbad (n) *swimming baths*
schwimmen *to swim*
schwindlig *dizzy, giddy*
schwitzen *to sweat*
schwül *sultry, oppressive, heavy (weather)*
See (m) *lake*
See (f) *sea*
seekrank *sea-sick*
Segelboot (n) *sailing boat*
segeln *to sail*
sehen *to see*
sehenswert *worth seeing*
Sehenswürdigkeit (f) *sight (beauty spot, etc)*
sehr *very*
sehr geehrter Herr *Dear Sir*
sehr gut *very good*
Seide (f) *silk*
Seife (f) *soap*
Seilbahn (f) *cable railway, funicular*
sein *to be*
Seite (f) *page*
Sekretär(-in) (m, f) *secretary*
Sekt (m) *(German) champagne*
Sekunde (f) *second*
selbst (one) *self/even*
Selbstbedienung (f) *self-service*
Selbsttanken (n) *self-service petrol*

Semester (n) *Term*
senden *to send; broadcast*
Sendung (f) *radio/tv programme*
Senf (m) *mustard*
September (m) *September*
Sessel (m) *arm-chair*
setzen (sich) *to sit down*
Shampoo (m) *shampoo*
sicher *sure, safe, secure*
Sicherheitsgurt (m) *safety-belt*
siezen *to call s.o.* Sie
Silber (n) *silver*
singen *to sing*
Single (m) *single person*
Single (f) *record*
Single (n) *tennis singles*
sitzen *to be sitting*
sitzenbleiben *to stay down a year (school, etc)*
Ski (m) *ski*
skifahren *to ski*
skilaufen *to ski*
Skistock *ski pole*
so *thus, so*
Socke (f) *sock*
sofort *immediately, straightaway*
sogar *even*
sogleich *immediately*
Sohn (m) *son*
Sommer (m) *Summer*
Sommerschlußverkauf (m) *summer-sale*
Sonderangebot (m) *special offer*
Sonderpreis (m) *special price*
Sonnabend (m) *Saturday*
Sonne (f) *sun*
Sonnenbrille (f) *sun-glasses*
Sonnencreme (f) *sun cream*
Sonnenmilch *sun cream*
Sonnenschein (m) *sunshine*
sonnig *sunny*
Sonntag (m) *Sunday*
sonst *otherwise; else*
Soße (f) *sauce, gravy*
Spanien (n) *Spain*
Spanier(-in) (m, f) *Spaniard*
spanisch *Spanish*
spannend *exciting, thrilling, tense*
sparen *to save*
Sparkasse (f) *savings bank*
spät *late*
spazieren gehen *to go for a walk*
Spaziergang (m) *walk*

Speisekarte (f) *menu*
Speisesaal (m) *dining-hall, dining-room (restaurant)*
Speisewagen (m) *dining-car*
Spiegel (m) *mirror*
Spiegelei (n) *fried egg*
Spiel (n) *game*
spielen *to play*
Spielzeug (n) *toy, plaything*
spitze! *great!, ace!*
Sport (m) *sport*
Sportplatz (m) *sports-field, playing-field*
Sprachlabor (n) *language laboratory*
sprechen *to speak*
Sprechstunde (f) *consulting hours*
springen *to jump, spring*
Spritze (f) *spray, nozzle, syringe*
Sprudel (m) *(fizzy) mineral water*
spülen *to rinse, wash (dishes)*
Spülmaschine (f) *dish-washer*
Spülmittel (n) *washing-up liquid, powder*
Staat (m) *State*
Staatsangehörigkeit (f) *nationality, citizenship*
Stadion (n) *stadium*
Stadt (f) *town*
Stadtmauer (f) *town (city) wall, boundary*
Stadmitte (f) *town centre*
Stadplan (m) *town map*
Stadtteil (m) *a part of town*
Stadzentrum (n) *town centre*
Stahl (m) *steel*
Stall (m) *stable, cowshed*
Stammtisch (m) *regulars' table*
stark *strong, powerful*
starten *to start*
Station (f) *(underground) station; terminus*
Stau (m) *tailback (traffic)*
Steak (m) *steak*
Steckdose (f) *electric socket, plug*
stecken *to put, fix, stick*
Stecker (m) *electric plug*
stehen *to stand*
Stehlampe (f) *standard lamp*
stehlen *to steal*
steil *steep*
Stein (m) *stone*
Stelle (f) *job, place, position*
stellen *to put, place*
sterben *to die*
Stereoanlage (f) *stereo system*

German–English Vocabulary 161

Stern (m) *star*
Stewardeß (f) *stewardess*
Stiefel (m) *boot*
still *still, quiet, calm*
stimmen *to agree, be right, tally*
Stock (m) *stick*
Stoff (m) *material*
Strafarbeit (f) *imposition (school)*
Strafe (f) *punishment*
Strand (m) *beach*
Straße (f) *street*
Straßenbahn (f) *tram, tramway*
Streichholz (n) *match*
streng *strict, hard*
stricken *to knit*
Strohhalm (m) *blade of straw, drinking straw*
Strom (m) *electric current, stream*
Strumpf (m) *stocking*
Strumpfhose (f) *tights*
Stück (n) *piece, item, each*
Student(-in) (m, f) *student*
studieren *to study*
Stuhl (m) *chair*
stumm *dumb, silent*
Stunde (f) *hour, lesson*
Stundenplan (m) *timetable*
Sturm (m) *storm*
stürmisch *stormy*
stürzen *to burst, collapse, fall, rush*
suchen *to search, look for*
Süd (m) *South*
Supermarkt (m) *supermarket*
Suppe (f) *soup, supper*
süß *sweet*
Sylvester (n) *New Year's Eve*
sympathisch *friendly, sympathetic*

T

T-shirt (n) *T-shirt*
Tabak (m) *tobacco*
Tablett (n) *tray*
Tablette (f) *tablet, pill, bar (chocolate)*
Tafel (f) *(black)board*
Tag (m) *day*
Tageskarte (f) *day's ticket; menu of the day*
täglich *daily*
Tal (n) *valley*
tanken *to put petrol in (the tank)*
Tankstelle (f) *filling-station*
Tante (f) *aunt*
tanzen *to dance*
Tasche (f) *pocket, satchel, case*
Taschenbuch (n) *paperback*
Taschendieb (m) *pickpocket*
Taschengeld (m) *pocket money*
Taschentuch (m) *handerkerchief*
Tasse (f) *cup*
Taste (f) *key, push-button*
taub *deaf*
tauchen *to drive*
Taxi (n) *taxi*
Tee (m) *tea*
Teekanne (f) *tea-pot*
TEE-Zug (m) *Trans-Europe-Express train*
Telefon (n) *telephone*
telefonieren *to telephone*
Telefonnummer (f) *phone number*
Telefonzelle (f) *phone booth*
Telegramm (n) *telegram*
Teller (m) *plate*
Tennis (n) *tennis*
Teppich (m) *carpet*
Termin (m) *date, appointment*
Terrasse (f) *terrace*
teuer *dear, expensive*
Theater (n) *theatre*
Theke (f) *bar, counter*
Thermometer (n) *thermometer*
tief *deep, low*
Tiefgarage (f) *underground car park*
Tiefsttemperatur (f) *minimum temperature*
Tier (n) *animal*
Tiger (m) *tiger*
Tisch (m) *table*
Tischtennis (n) *table-tennis*
Tochter (f) *daughter*
Tod (m) *death*
Toilette (f) *toilet*
Toilettenpapier (n) *toilet paper*
toll *wild, terrific, fantastic*
Tomate (f) *tomato*
Tonbandgerät (n) *tape-recorder*
Topf (m) *pot, pan*
Tor (n) *gate, goal*
Torte (f) *tart*
tot *dead*
tragbar *portable*
tragen *to carry, wear*
trainieren (sich) *to train*
Trainingsanzug (m) *track suit*

trampen *to hitch-hike*
Transistor (m) *transistor*
Traube (f) *grape*
treffen (sich) *to meet*
Treffpunkt (m) *meeting place, rendez-vous*
treiben *to do (sport)*
Treppe (f) *step, stair*
trimmen (sich) *to get fit*
trinken *to drink*
trocken *dry*
trocknen *to dry*
Trompete (f) *trumpet*
Tropfen (m) *drop*
trüb *overcast, gloomy, dismal*
Tschüß *Bye now!, Ta-Ta!, So long!*
tun *to do, put*
Turm (m) *tower*
turnen *to do gymnastics*
Turnhalle (f) *gymnasium*
Tür (f) *door*
Tüte (f) *(paper, plastic) bag*
typisch *typical*

U
u.a. *amongst others*
U-bahn (f) *underground, tube*
übel *wicked, nasty, evil*
üben *to practise*
über Bonn *via Bonn*
überall *everywhere*
überfahren *to run over, drive through, drive across*
Überfahrt (f) *crossing*
überfallen *to attack, hold up*
übergeben (sich) *to be sick*
überholen *to overtake, pass*
übermorgen *the day after tomorrow*
übernachten *to spend the night*
Übernachtung (f) *overnight stay*
überqueren *to cross (street)*
überraschen *to surprise*
Überraschung (f) *surprise*
übersetzen *to translate*
Ufer (n) *shore, bank*
Uhr (f) *time, watch, clock*
Uhrzeit (f) *time by the watch (clock)*
Umkleideraum (m) *changing room*
umkommen *to die, be killed*
Umleitung (f) *detour*
Umschlag (m) *envelope, dust jacket*
umsonst *for nothing, in vain*
umsteigen *to change (trains, etc)*

Umtausch (m) *exchange*
umtauschen *to exchange*
umziehen (sich) *to get changed*
unentschieden *undecided, drawn (game)*
Unfall (m) *accident*
unfit *unfit, out of condition*
unfreundlich *unfriendly*
ungefähr *about, approximately*
ungenügend *unsatisfactory*
Uni (f) *uni(versity)*
Universität (f) *university*
unmöglich *impossible*
unten *below*
Untergeschoß (n) *basement*
Unterkunft (f) *accommodation*
Unterricht (m) *teaching, tuition*
unterschreiben *to sign*
Unterschrift (f) *signature*
untersuchen *to investigate*
Untertasse (f) *saucer*
Unterwäsche (f) *underwear*
Urlaub (m) *holiday(s)*
usw *etc*

V
Vanille (f) *vanilla*
Vater (m) *father*
Vati *dad, daddy*
Verabredung (f) *appointment, date*
verabschieden (sich) *to depart, take one's leave*
Verband (m) *association*
verbessern *to improve, correct*
verbinden *to connect*
Verbindung (f) *connection*
verboten *forbidden, prohibited, not allowed*
verbringen *to spend (time)*
Verein (m) *club*
(die) Vereinigten Staaten (pl.) *United States*
verfahren (sich) *to get lost, lose one's way*
vergessen *to forget*
verheiratet *married*
verirren (sich) *to get lost*
verkaufen *to sell*
Verkäufer(-in) (m, f) *sales person*
Verkehr (m) *traffic*
verkehren *to run (bus, train, etc)*
Verkehrsamt (n) *Tourist information office*
Verkehrsstauung (f) *traffic-jam, hold-up*

German–English Vocabulary

verlassen *to leave*
verlaufen (sich) *to get lost*
verletzt *injured, wounded*
verlieren *to lose*
verlobt *engaged*
Verlobte(-r) (f, m) *fiancée, fiancé*
verpassen *to miss (train, etc)*
verreisen *to go off (on a journey)*
verschließen *to lock, bolt*
verschwinden *to disappear*
versetzen *to move, transfer*
versichern *to insure*
verspätet *late*
Verspätung (f) *lateness*
verstehen *to understand*
Verstopfung (f) *constipation*
versuchen *to attempt, try*
verunglücken *to have an accident*
Verwandte(-r) (m, f) *relative, relation*
verwundet *injured, wounded*
verzeihen *to excuse, pardon*
Verzeihung! *Excuse me!, Pardon me!*
verzollen *to declare (customs)*
Vetter (m) *cousin (male)*
Videogerät (n) *video-machine*
Vieh (n) *cattle, beasts*
viel *much*
viel Glück! *good luck!*
viel Spaß! *have fun!*
viel Vergnügen! *enjoy yourself!*
viele *many*
vielen Dank! *thanks very much!*
vielleicht *perhaps*
Viertel (n) *quarter*
Vogel (m) *bird*
voll *full*
Volleyball (m) *volleyball*
Vollpension (f) *full-board*
volltanken *to fill up (with petrol)*
vorbereiten *to prepare*
Vorfahrt (f) *right of way*
vorgehen *to go in front of*
vorhaben *to have on, have planned*
Vorhang (m) *curtain*
vorig- *previous*
Vormittag (m) *before noon*
vormittags *in the morning*
Vorname (m) *Christian/first name*
vorne *in front, ahead*
Vorort (m) *suburb*
vorschlagen *to suggest*
Vorsicht! *Watch out!, Careful!*

Vorspeise (f) *starter (course at meal)*
vorstellen (sich) *to imagine*
Vorstellung (f) *imagination*
Vorwahlnummer (f) *dialling code*
vorzeigen *to produce, show (ticket, passport, etc)*
vorziehen *to prefer*

W

wach *awake*
wachsen *to grow*
Wagen (m) *car, vehicle, waggon, coach*
Wahl (f) *choice*
wählen *to choose, dial*
Wahlfach (n) *optional subject*
Wald (m) *wood*
Wand (f) *wall*
wandern *to hike, ramble*
Wanderung (f) *hike, (long) country walk*
Warenhaus (n) *department store*
warm *warm*
Warnung (f) *warning*
warten *to wait*
Warteraum (m) *waiting-room*
Wartesaal (m) *waiting-room*
was für *what kind of*
Waschbecken (n) *wash-basin*
Wäsche (f) *washing, laundry, underwear*
waschen (sich) *to wash (o.s.)*
Wäscherei (f) *laundry*
Waschmaschine (f) *washing machine*
Waschpulver (n) *washing powder*
Waschraum (m) *washroom*
Wasser (n) *water*
Wasserball (m) *water polo*
Wasserhahn (m) *tap*
Wechsel (m) *change; bureau de change*
wechseln *to change*
Wechselstube (f) *exchange office*
wecken *to wake*
Wecker (m) *alarm clock*
Weg (m) *way; path*
weg *away*
Wegweiser (m) *signpost*
wegwerfen *to throw away*
wehtun *to hurt*
weiblich *female, feminine*
Weihnachten (f) *Christmas*
Weile (f) *while*
Wein (m) *wine*
weinen *to cry*
Weinliste (f) *wine-list*

Weintraube (f) *grape*
weiß *white*
Weißwein (m) *white wine*
weit *far*
Wellensittich (m) *budgie*
Weltmeisterschaften (f/pl.) *world championship*
wenig *little, not much*
werden *to become*
werfen *to throw*
Werkstatt (f) *workshop, repair garage*
werktags *weekdays, working days*
West (m) *West*
Wetter (n) *weather*
Wetterbericht (m) *weather report*
Wettervorhersage (f) *weather forecast*
wie *how*
wieso *why, how come*
wie bitte? *pardon?*
wieviel(e) *how much/many*
wieder *again*
wiederholen *to repeat*
wiegen *to weigh*
Wien *Vienna*
Wiener Schnitzel *veal escalope*
Wiese (f) *meadow*
Wildleder (n) *suede*
willkommen *welcome*
Wind (m) *wind*
windig *windy*
Windschutzscheibe (f) *windscreen*
Winter (m) *winter*
wirklich *really*
Wirtschaft (f) *economy, housekeeping*
Wirtshaus (n) *(approx) public house (n)*
wissen *to know*
Witwe (f) *widow*
wo . . . her *from where*
Woche (f) *week*
Wochenende (n) *weekend*
wochentags *weekdays*
wöchentlich *weekly*
woher *from where*
wohnen *to live*
Wohnort (m) *(place of) residence*
Wohnung (f) *flat, apartment*
Wohnwagen (m) *caravan*
Wohnzimmer (n) *living room*
wolkig *cloudy*
Wolle (f) *wool*
Wort (n) *word*
Wörterbuch (n) *dictionary*
Wunde (f) *wound, injury*

wunderbar *wonderful*
wünschen *to wish*
Wurst (f) *sausage*

Z
zahlen *to pay*
Zahn (m) *tooth*
Zahnarzt(-in) (m, f) *dentist*
Zahnbürste (f) *toothbrush*
Zahnpasta (f) *toothpaste*
z.B. *e.g.*
zeichnen *to draw*
zeigen *to show*
Zeit (f) *time*
Zeitschrift (f) *periodical*
Zeitung (f) *newspaper*
Zelt (n) *tent*
zelten *to camp*
Zentimeter (m) *centimetre*
Zentralheizung *central heating*
Zettel (m) *slip of paper*
Zeuge (m) *witness*
Zeugnis (n) *account, evidence, testimony*
ziehen *to draw, pull*
ziemlich *rather, quite*
Zigarette (f) *cigarette*
Zigarre (f) *cigar*
Zimmer (n) *room*
Zitrone (f) *lemon*
Zoll (m) *customs*
zollfrei *duty-free*
Zollkontrolle (f) *customs examination*
Zoo (m) *zoo*
zu Fuß *on foot*
zu Mittag essen *to have lunch/dinner*
Zucker (m) *sugar*
zuerst *(at) first*
Zufahrt (f) *access*
zufrieden *satisfied, contented*
Zug (m) *train*
zuhören *to listen*
zumachen *to close*
Zunge (f) *tongue*
zusammen *together*
Zusammenstoß (m) *crash, collision*
Zuschauer(-in) (m, f) *bystander, spectator, member of audience*
Zuschlag (m) *supplement(-ary payment), surcharge*
zuschlagspflichtig *liable to surcharge*
Zwiebel (f) *onion*
zwo *two (on phone, etc)*